Bizarro
BUCCANEERS

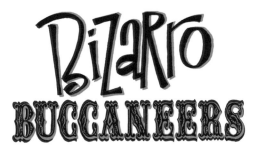

NUTTIN' BUT PIRATE CARTOONS

by Dan Piraro

Andrews McMeel Publishing, LLC

Kansas City

Bizarro Buccaneers copyright © 2008 by Dan Piraro. All rights reserved. Printed in Malaysia. No part of this book may be used or reproduced in any manner whatsoever without written permission except in the case of reprints in the context of reviews. For information, write Andrews McMeel Publishing, LLC, an Andrews McMeel Universal company, 1130 Walnut Street, Kansas City, Missouri 64106.

08 09 10 11 12 TWP 10 9 8 7 6 5 4 3 2 1

ISBN-13: 978-0-7407-7740-0
ISBN-10: 0-7407-7740-8

Library of Congress Control Number: 2008924726

www.andrewsmcmeel.com

ATTENTION: SCHOOLS AND BUSINESSES

For my favorite wench, Ashley,
for whom I would gladly walk the plank.
Unless doing so would result in serious injury or death,
in which case what would really be the point of that?

Foreword

I promised myself I would not begin this foreword with something lame like, *"Avast, ye scurvy knaves!"* and I am a man of my word. Pirates, on the other hand, were not.

In reality, these outlaws were brutal, filthy, lying, flea-infested, lice-ridden, murdering, thieving, slave-trading, scum of the earth. Yet now they are among our favorite sexy heroes. It makes me wonder if amusement parks and films in the next couple of centuries will glorify earth's current ruthless dictators, serial killers, and corporate criminals. Will there one day be a series of Hollywood blockbusters with Jeffrey Dahmer or Ken Lay as the romantic hero?

But for now, enjoy this book of scoundrels, malefactors, and miscreants of the past from the safety of the twenty-first century.

The cartoons herein are arranged in chronological order, so those in the first few pages are from the earliest days of *Bizarro*—the latter half of the 1980s. As such, the sight of them causes me great personal pain. My cartooning skills at the time—both literary and artistic—were brutish and it hurts me to look at them. Additionally, the older ones were drawn before cartoons were commonly posted on the Internet, so they were not colored. I colored them for this book, however, which means they have an old-style look to the line but a very recent approach to the color. You may not notice the difference, but to me it's like time travel.

One last note before you begin: Most cartoonists won't admit this, but one reason we love to draw pirate cartoons is that it is the only way we can get away with a joke about a disability in the newspaper's comics section. (I even refer to this principle in the cartoon on page 61.) If you draw a couple of shoppers at Wal-Mart with missing eyes, hook hands, and peg legs, people feel sorry for them and it ruins the joke. In fact, editors will foresee a day lost to answering angry e-mails and phone calls and may not even run the gag. With a pirate, however, any missing body parts are fair game and funny as hell.

Dan Piraro, Brooklyn, 2008

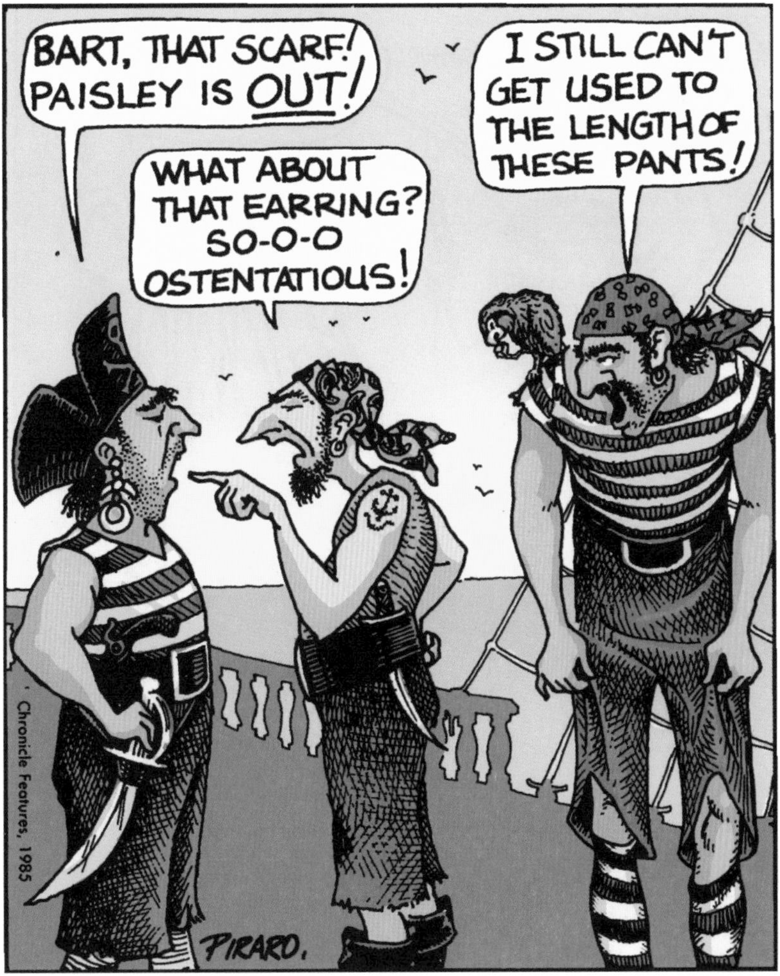
BART, THAT SCARF! PAISLEY IS OUT!
WHAT ABOUT THAT EARRING? SO-O-O OSTENTATIOUS!
I STILL CAN'T GET USED TO THE LENGTH OF THESE PANTS!
Chronicle Features, 1985
PIRARO.

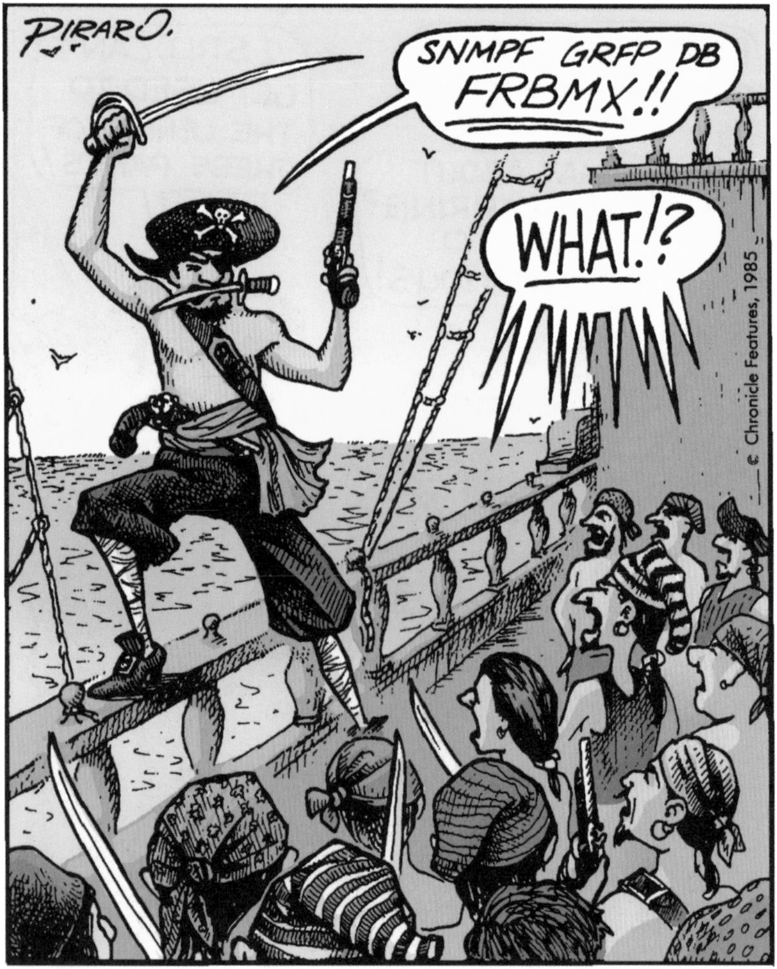
PIRARO.
SNMPF GRFP DB FRBMX!!
WHAT!?
© Chronicle Features, 1985

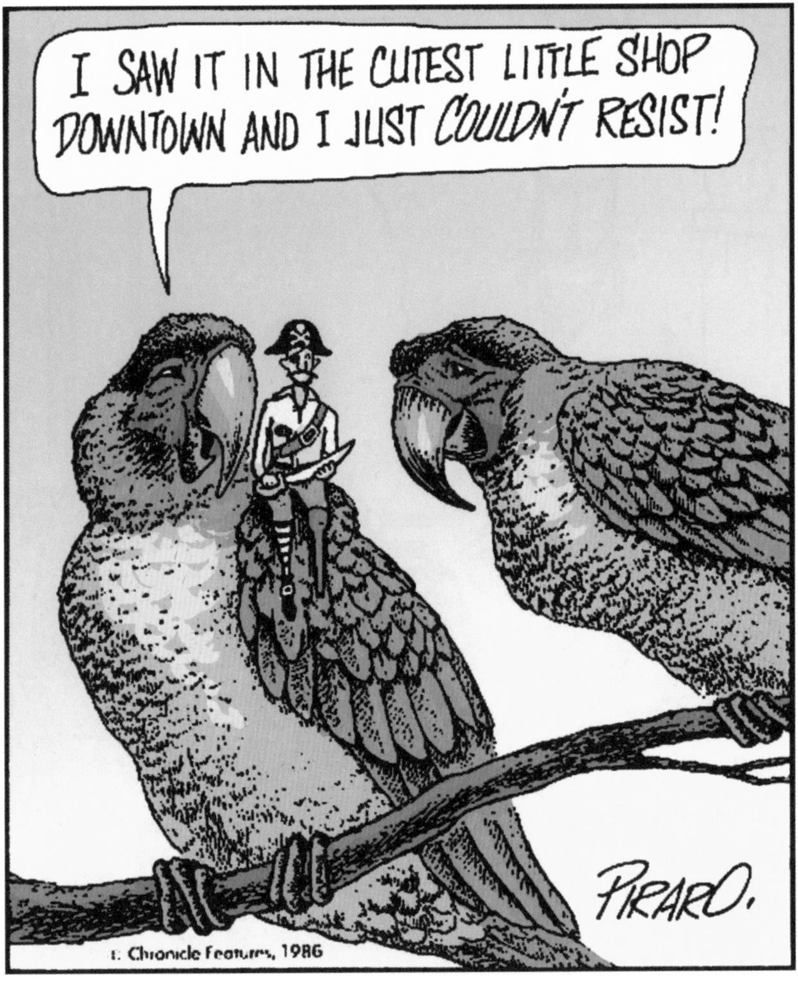
I SAW IT IN THE CUTEST LITTLE SHOP DOWNTOWN AND I JUST COULDN'T RESIST!
PIRARO.
© Chronicle Features, 1986

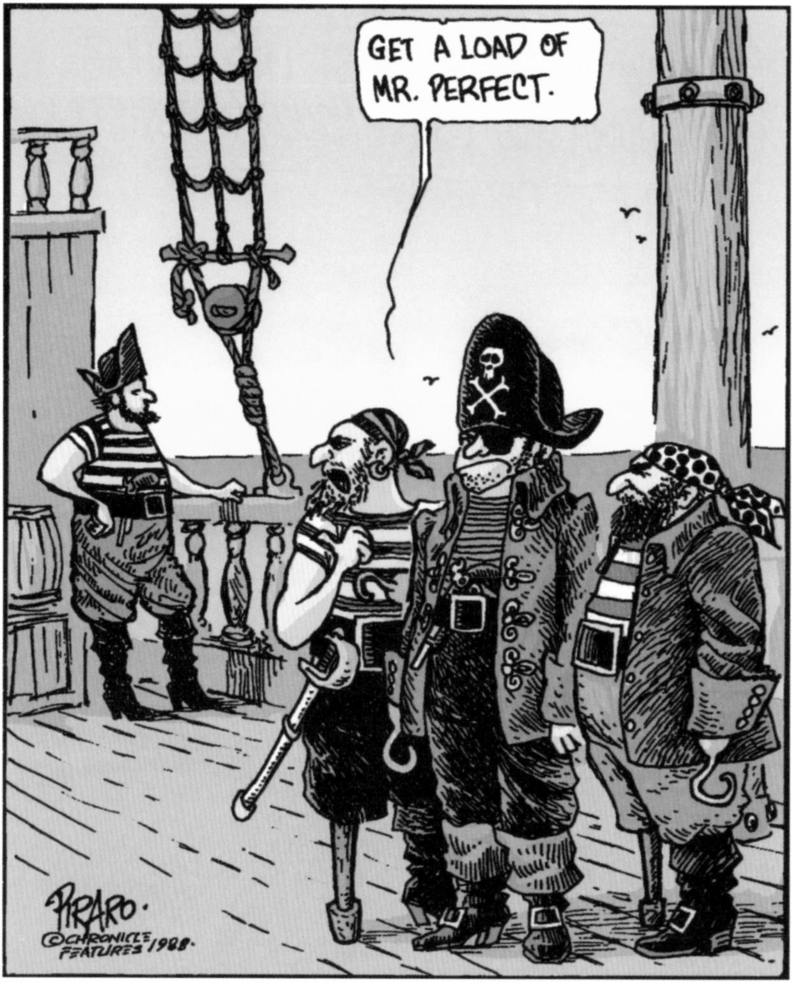
GET A LOAD OF MR. PERFECT.
PIRARO.
©CHRONICLE FEATURES 1988.

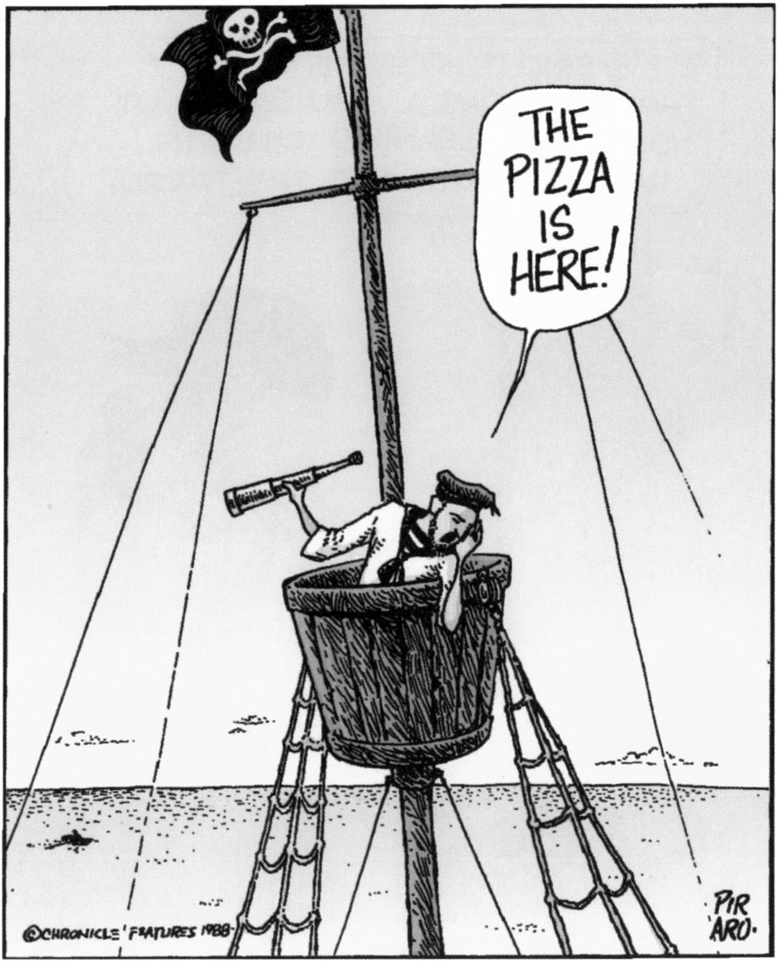
THE PIZZA IS HERE!
©CHRONICLE FEATURES 1988
PIRARO

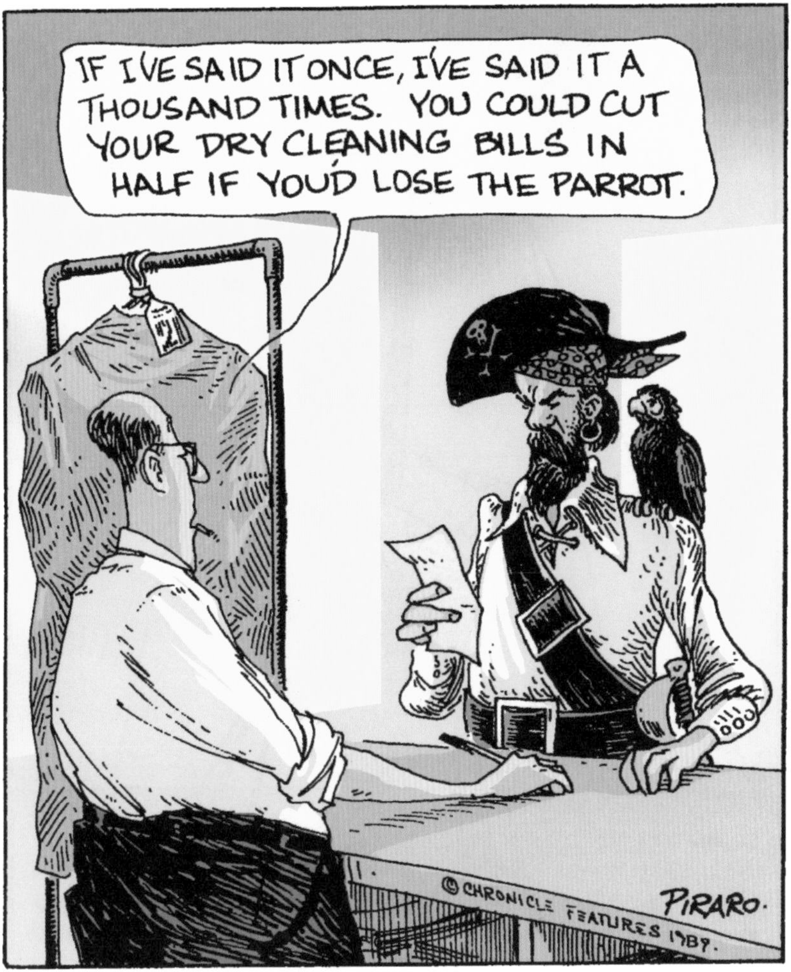
IF I'VE SAID IT ONCE, I'VE SAID IT A THOUSAND TIMES. YOU COULD CUT YOUR DRY CLEANING BILLS IN HALF IF YOU'D LOSE THE PARROT.
#2
© CHRONICLE FEATURES 1989.
PIRARO.

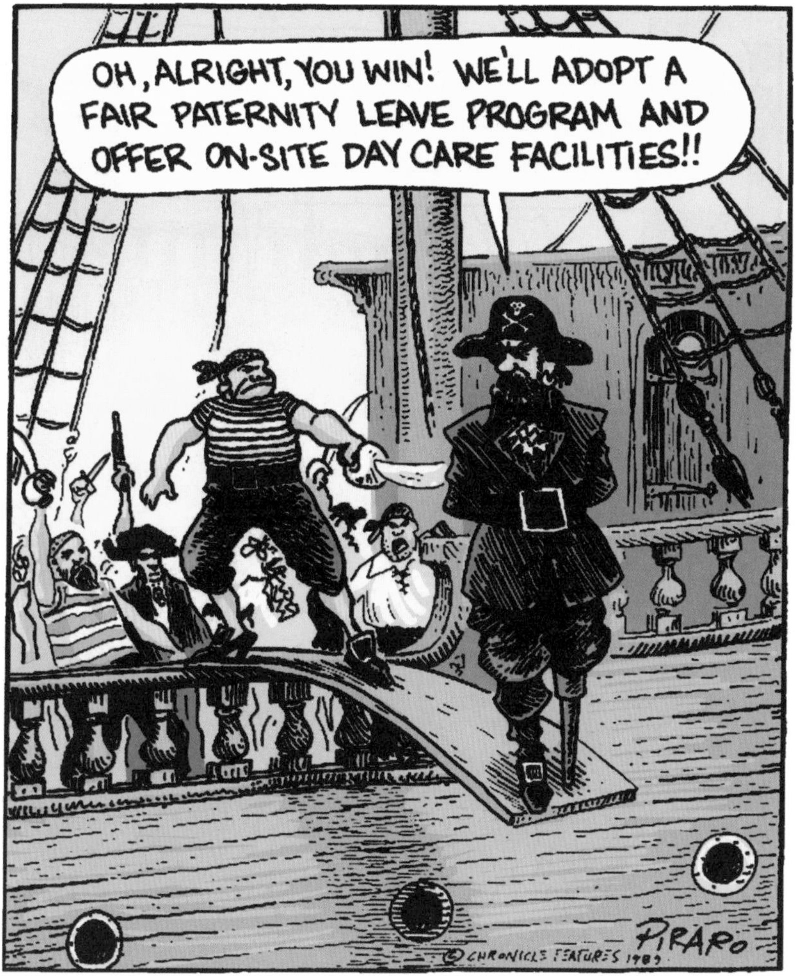
OH, ALRIGHT, YOU WIN! WE'LL ADOPT A FAIR PATERNITY LEAVE PROGRAM AND OFFER ON-SITE DAY CARE FACILITIES!!
PIRARO
© CHRONICLE FEATURES 1989

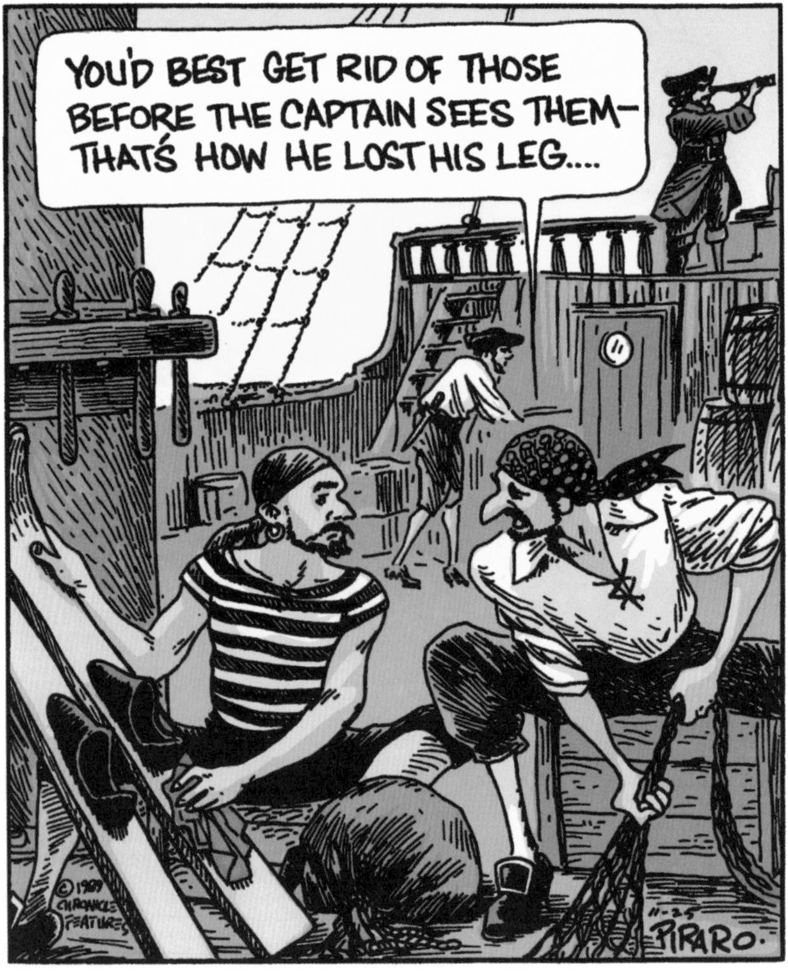
YOU'D BEST GET RID OF THOSE BEFORE THE CAPTAIN SEES THEM— THAT'S HOW HE LOST HIS LEG....
© 1989 CHRONICLE FEATURES
11-25
PIRARO.

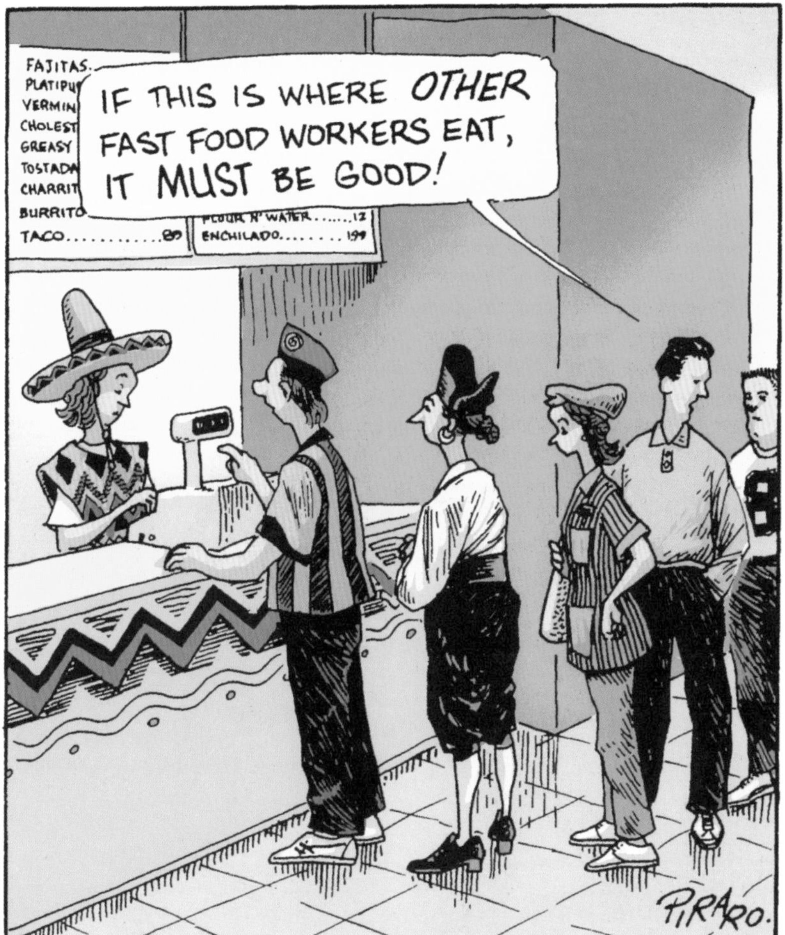
FAJITAS
PLATIPU
VERMIN
CHOLEST
GREASY
TOSTADA
CHARRIT
BURRITO
TACO..........89
FLOUR N' WATER......12
ENCHILADO........199
IF THIS IS WHERE *OTHER* FAST FOOD WORKERS EAT, IT MUST BE GOOD!
PIRARO.
©CHRONICLE FEATURES 1990.

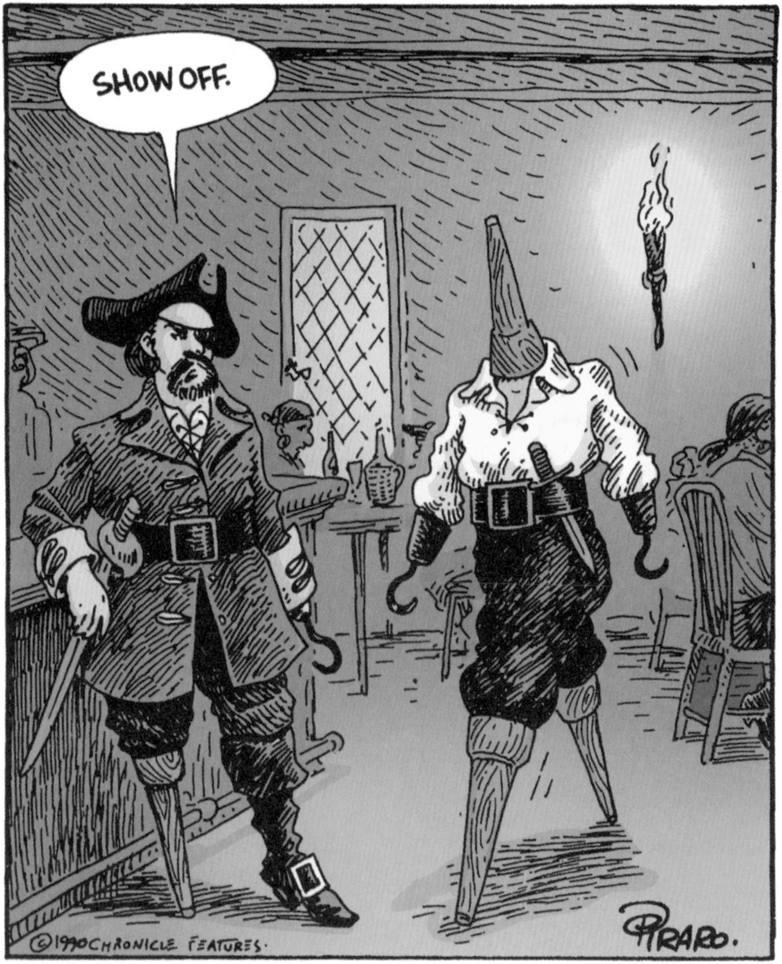
SHOW OFF.
©1990 CHRONICLE FEATURES.
PIRARO.

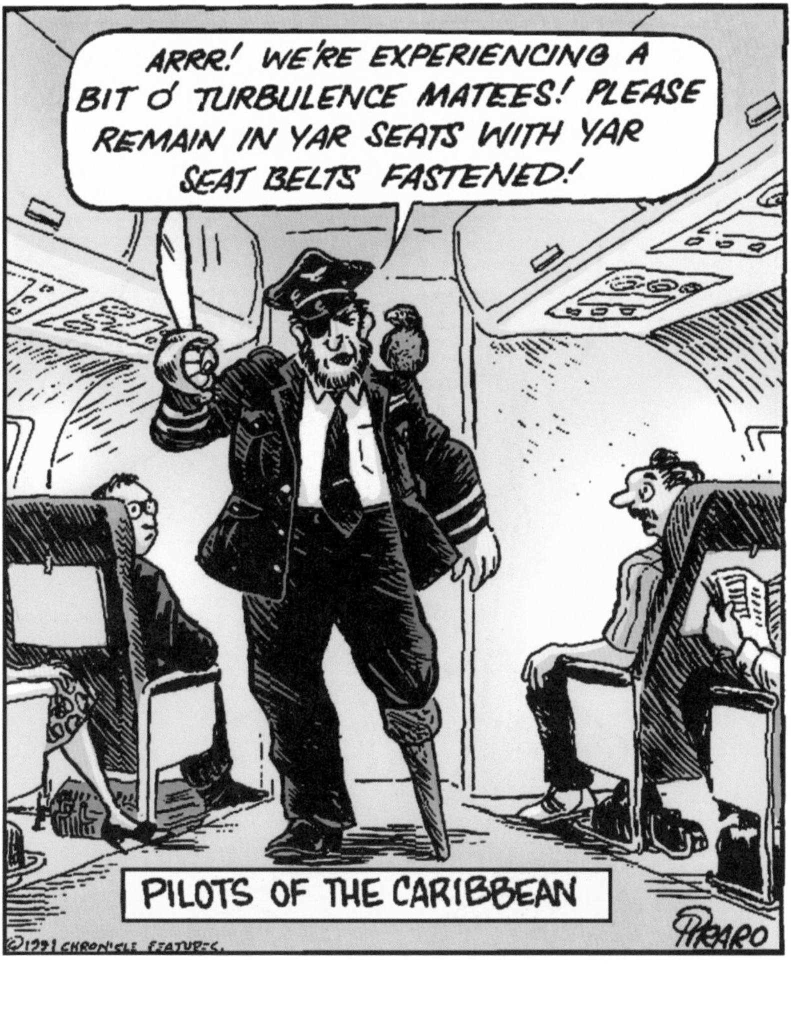
ARRR! WE'RE EXPERIENCING A BIT O' TURBULENCE MATEES! PLEASE REMAIN IN YAR SEATS WITH YAR SEAT BELTS FASTENED!
PIRARO
PILOTS OF THE CARIBBEAN

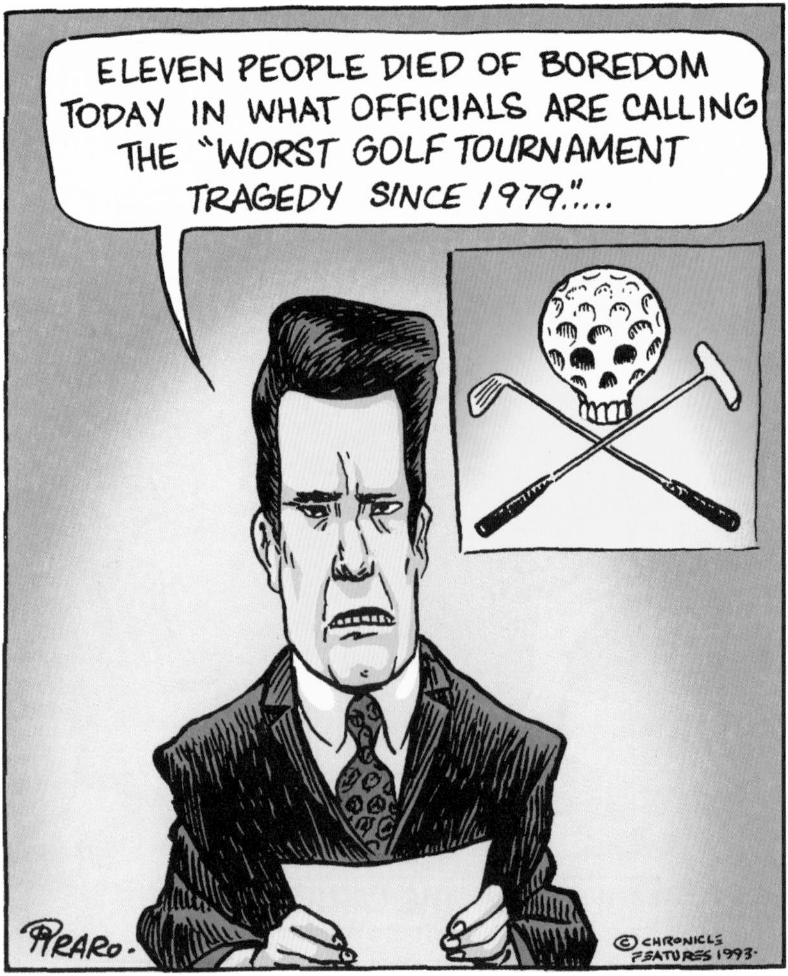
ELEVEN PEOPLE DIED OF BOREDOM TODAY IN WHAT OFFICIALS ARE CALLING THE "WORST GOLF TOURNAMENT TRAGEDY SINCE 1979."....
PIRARO.
© CHRONICLE FEATURES 1993.

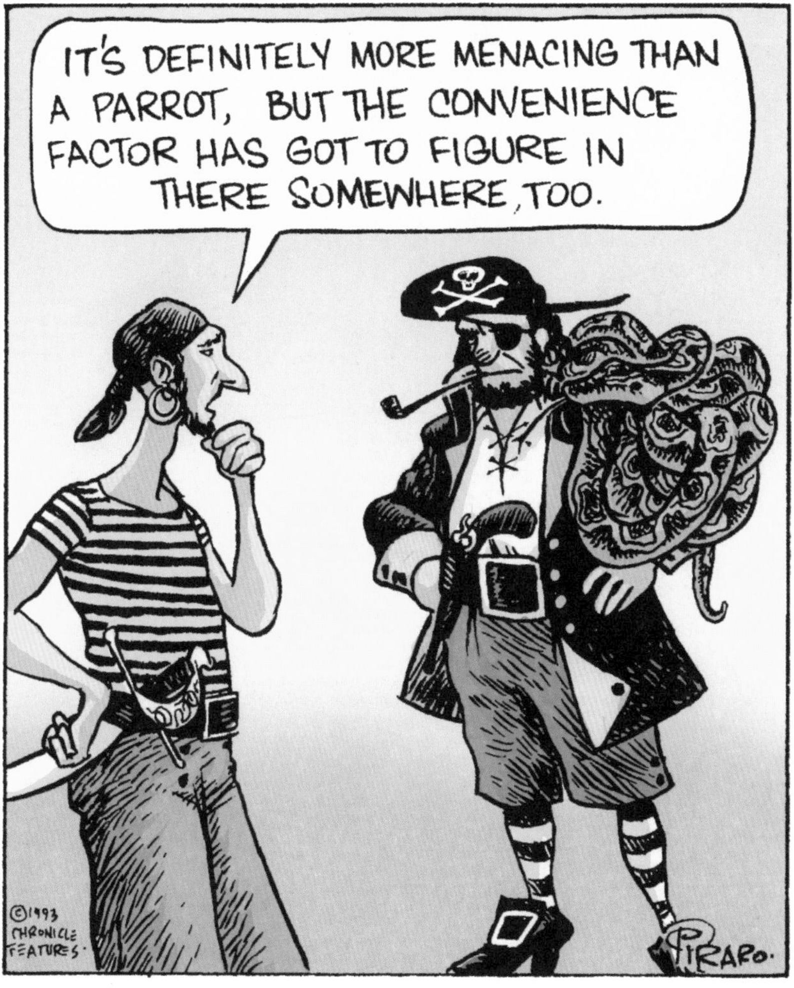
IT'S DEFINITELY MORE MENACING THAN A PARROT, BUT THE CONVENIENCE FACTOR HAS GOT TO FIGURE IN THERE SOMEWHERE, TOO.
©1993 CHRONICLE FEATURES
PIRARO.

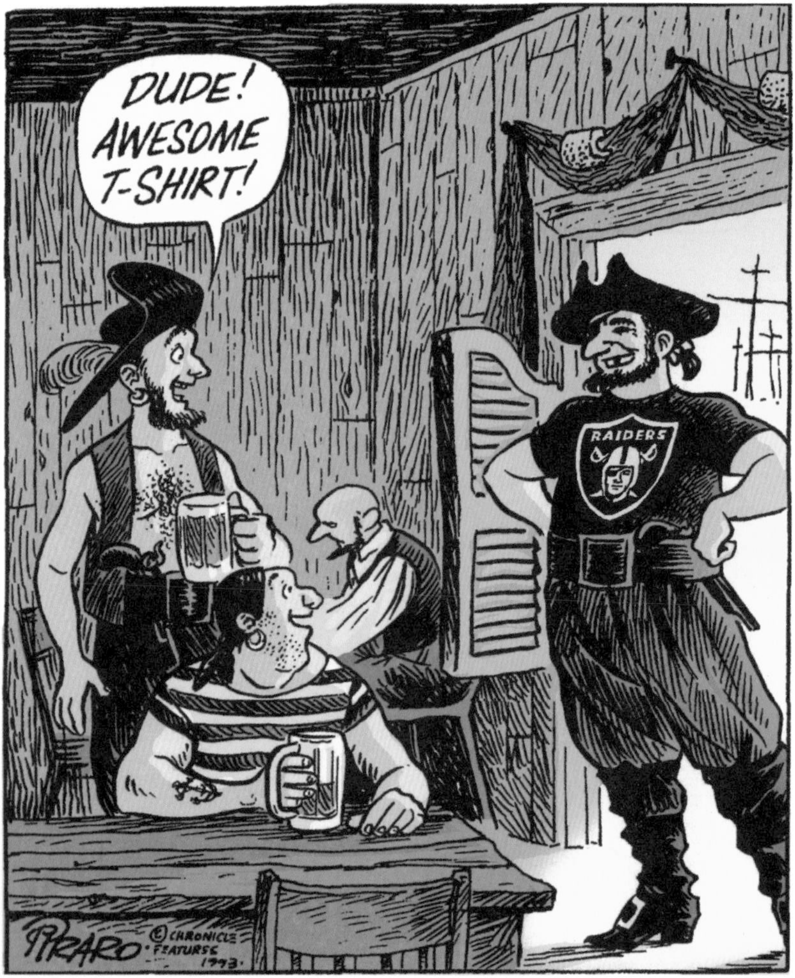
DUDE! AWESOME T-SHIRT!
RAIDERS
PIRARO © CHRONICLE FEATURES 1993

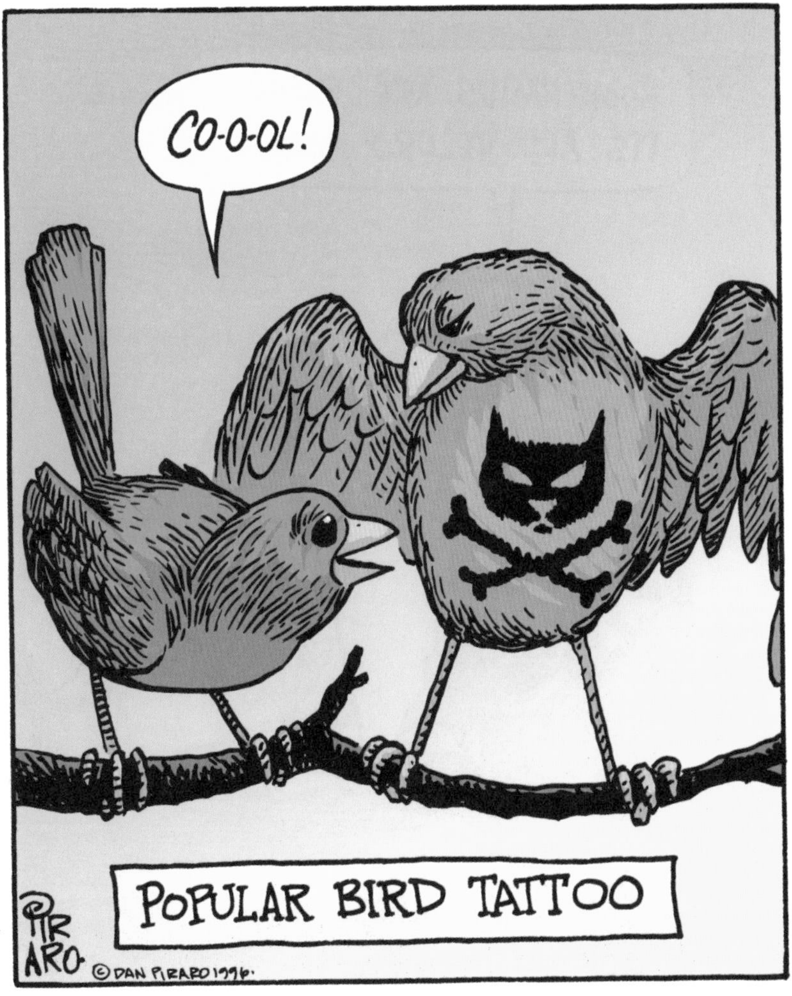
CO-O-OL!
POPULAR BIRD TATTOO
PIRARO
© DAN PIRARO 1996.

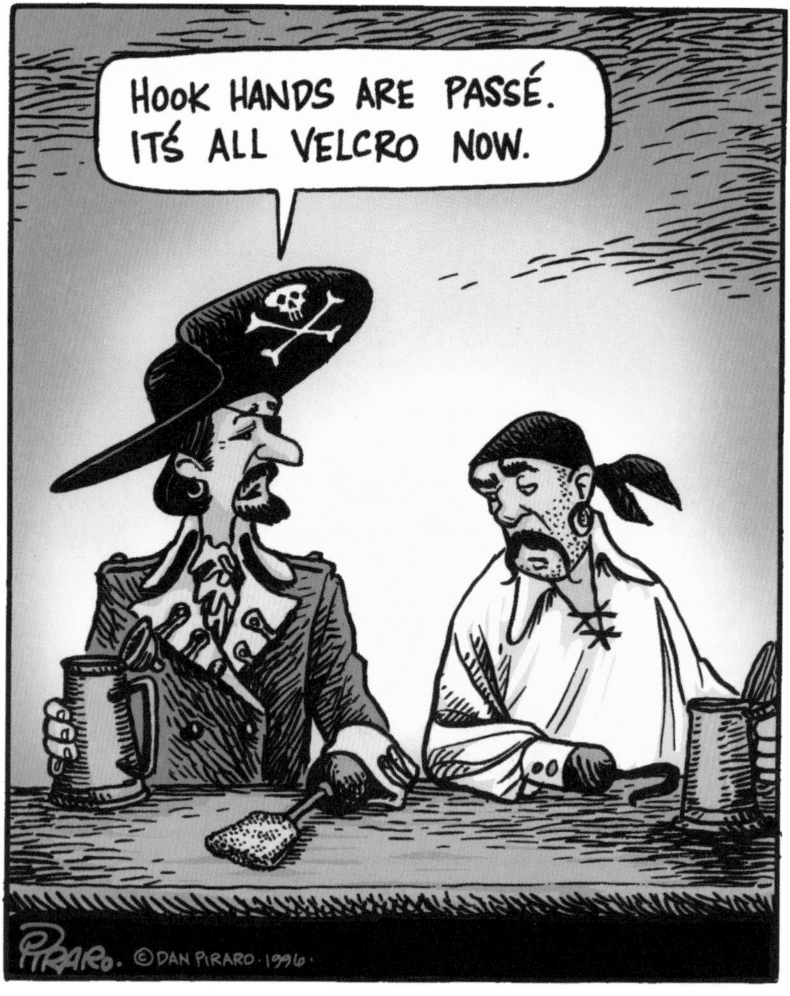
HOOK HANDS ARE PASSÉ. ITS ALL VELCRO NOW.
PIRARO. ©DAN PIRARO·1996·

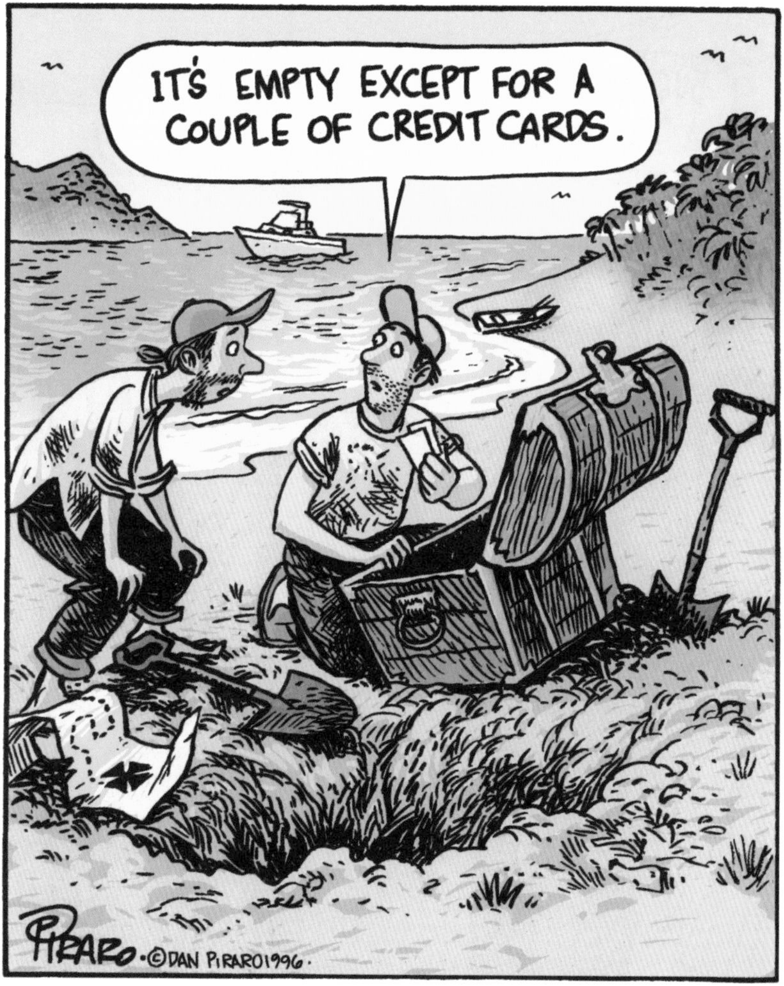
IT'S EMPTY EXCEPT FOR A COUPLE OF CREDIT CARDS.
PIRARO. ©DAN PIRARO 1996.

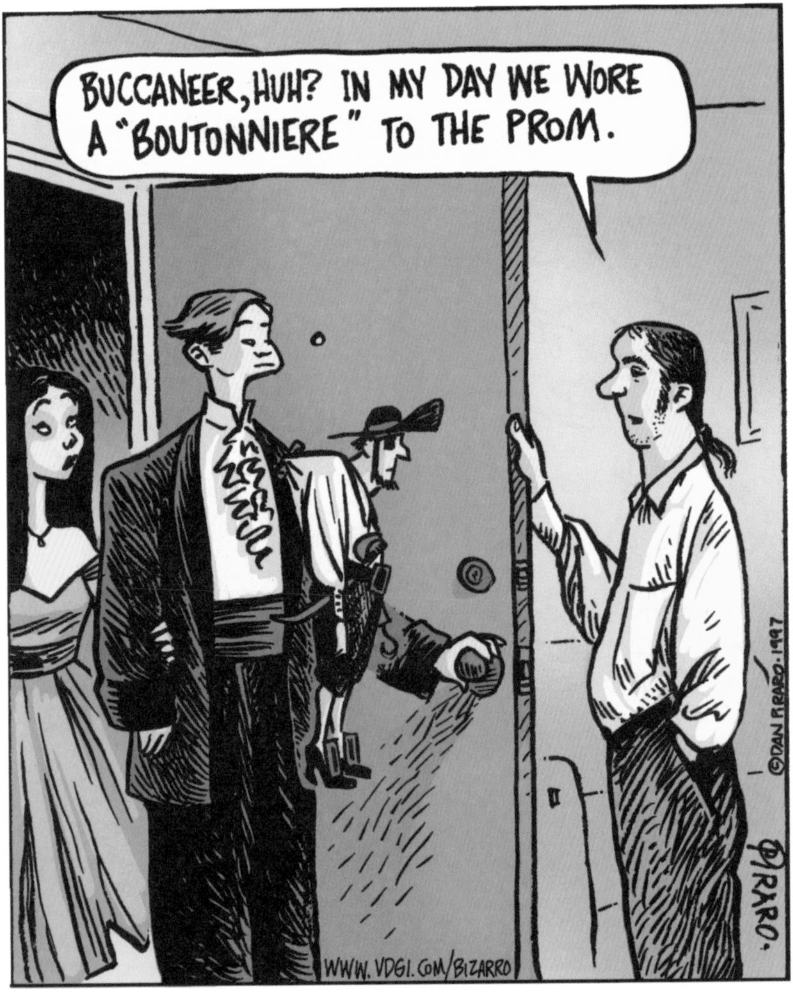
BUCCANEER, HUH? IN MY DAY WE WORE A "BOUTONNIERE" TO THE PROM.
©DAN PIRARO·1997
PIRARO.
WWW.VDGI.COM/BIZARRO

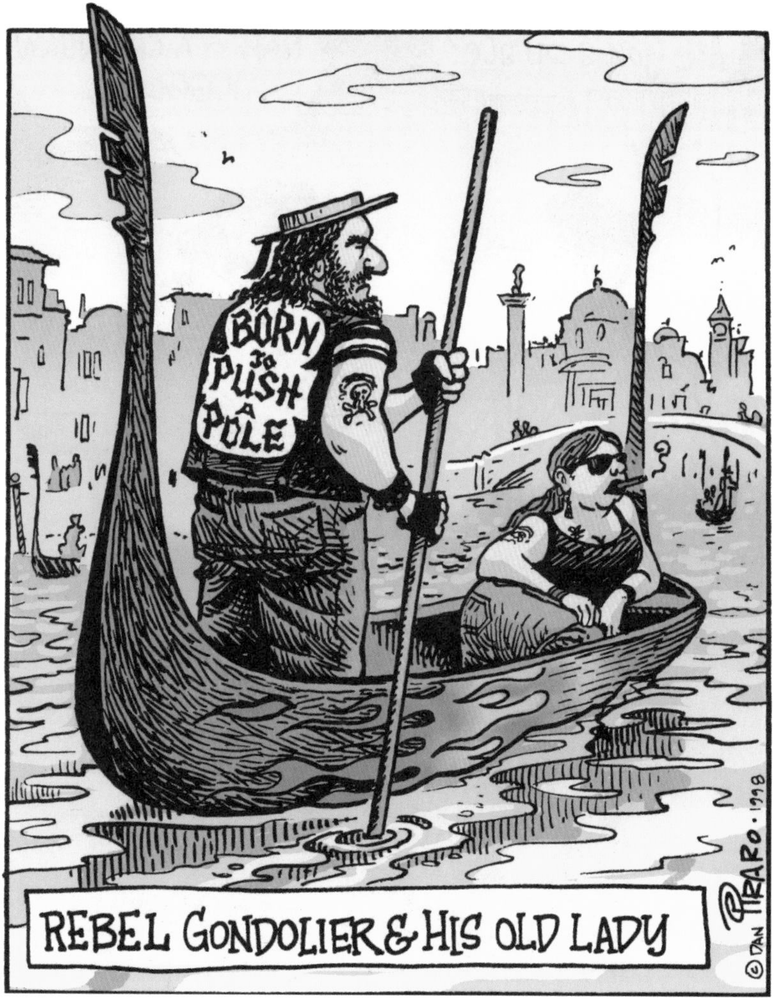
BORN to PUSH A POLE
© DAN PIRARO · 1998
REBEL GONDOLIER & HIS OLD LADY

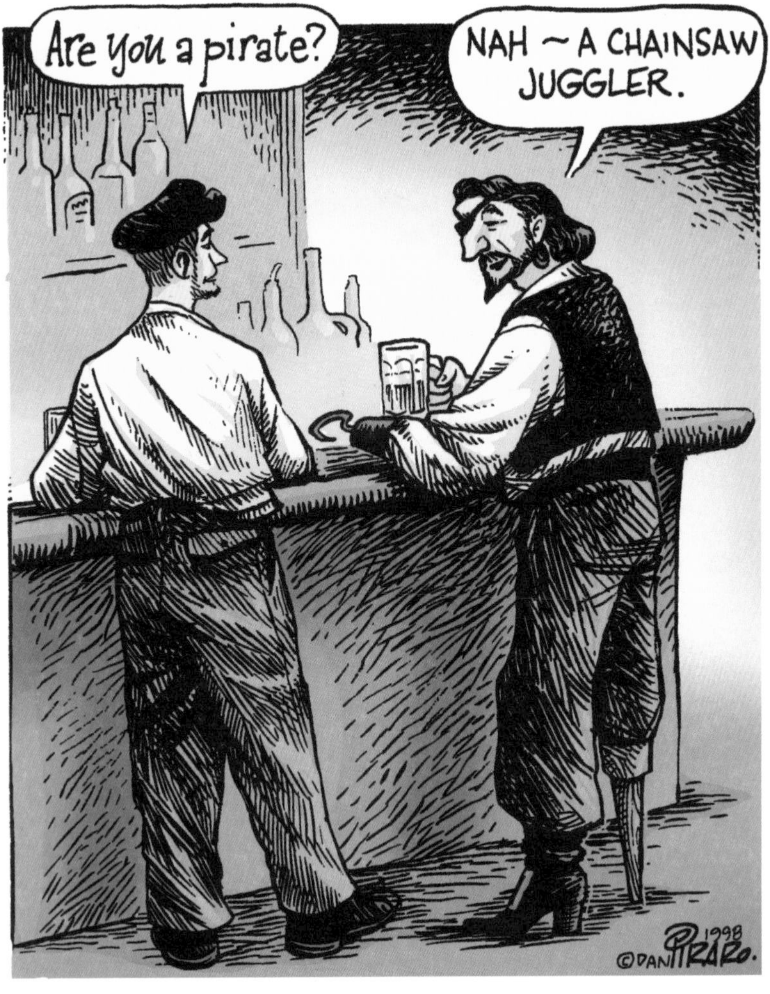
Are you a pirate?
NAH ~ A CHAINSAW JUGGLER.
1998 ©DAN PIRARO.

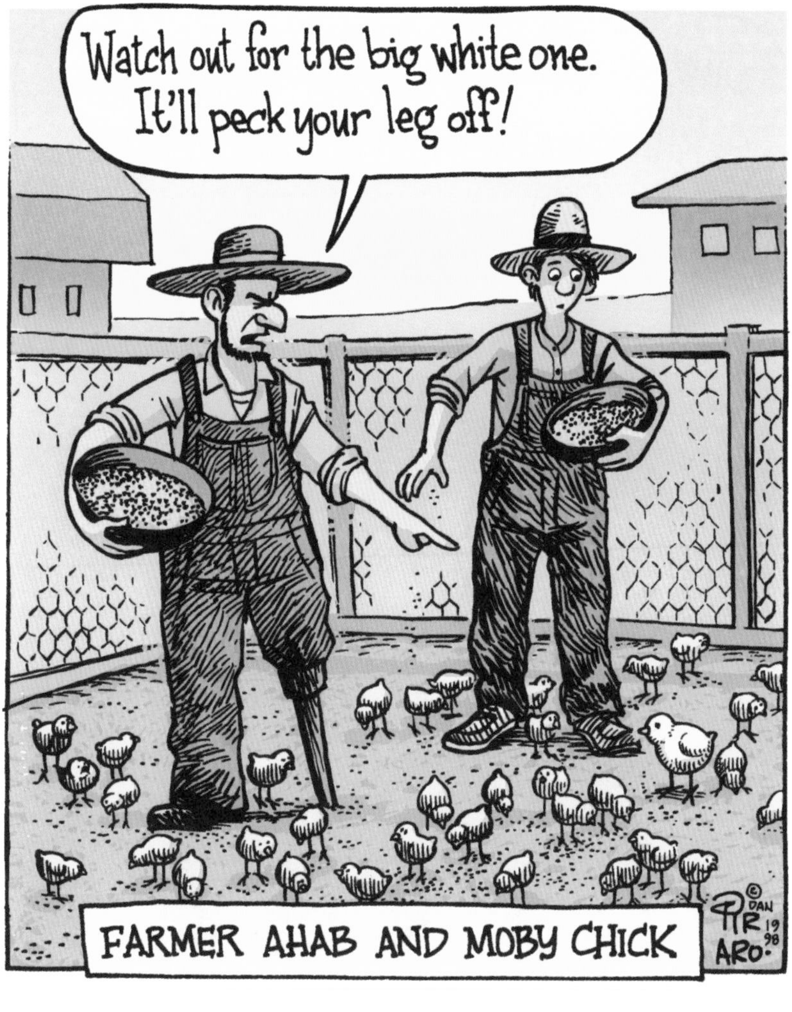
Watch out for the big white one. It'll peck your leg off!
FARMER AHAB AND MOBY CHICK
© DAN PIRARO 1998

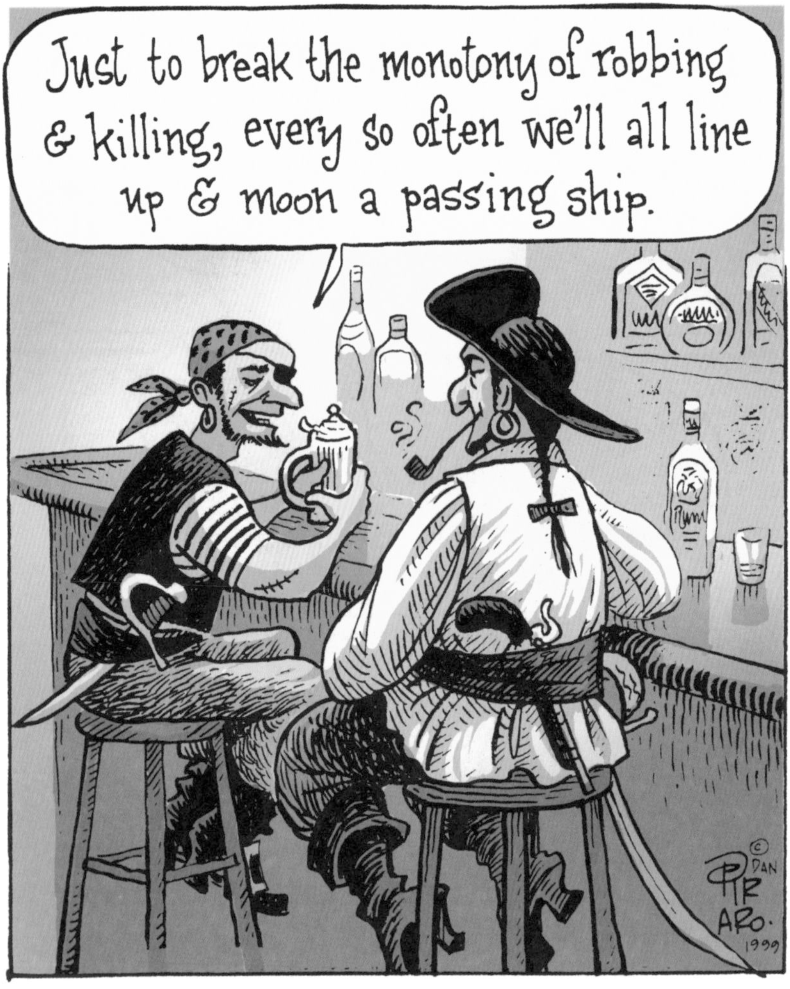
Just to break the monotony of robbing & killing, every so often we'll all line up & moon a passing ship.
Rum
© DAN PIRARO 1999

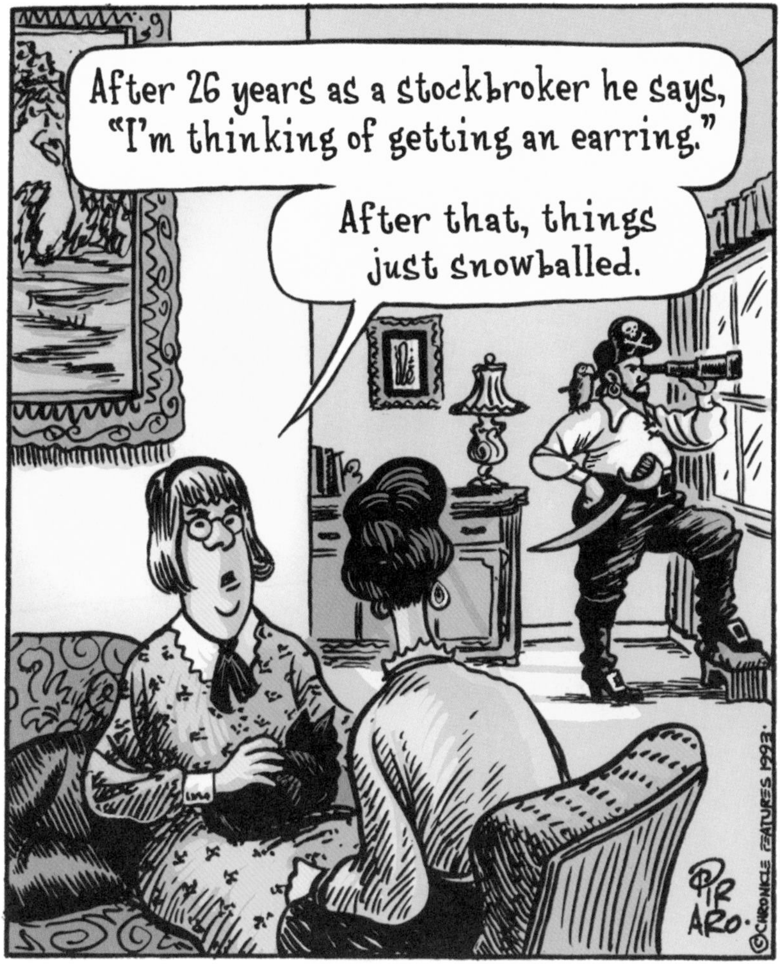
After 26 years as a stockbroker he says, "I'm thinking of getting an earring."
After that, things just snowballed.
PIRARO.
©CHRONICLE FEATURES 1993.

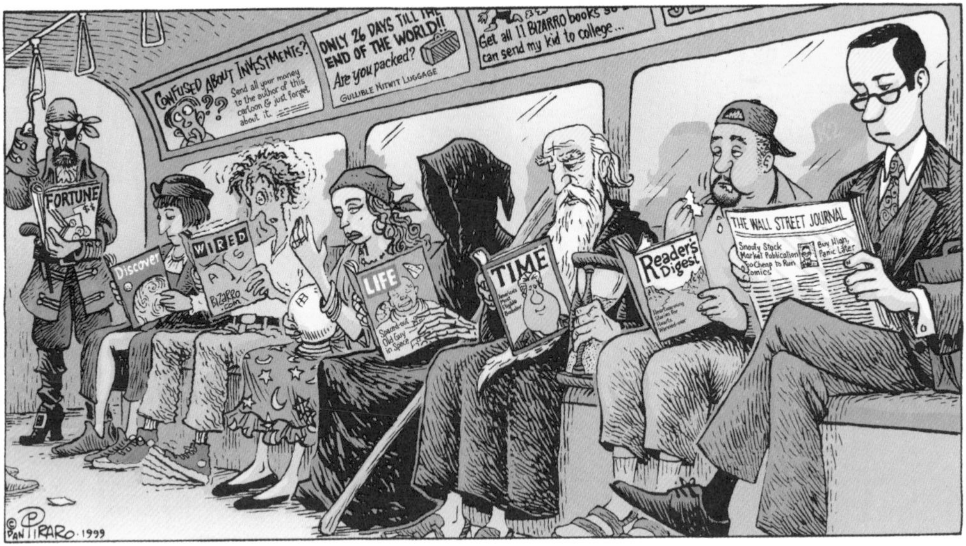
CONFUSED ABOUT INVESTMENTS?
Send all your money to the author of this cartoon & just forget about it.
ONLY 26 DAYS TILL THE END OF THE WORLD!!
Are you packed?
GULLIBLE NITWIT LUGGAGE
Get all 11 BIZARRO books so I can send my kid to college...
FORTUNE
Discover
WIRED
BIZARRO .com
LIFE
Spaced-out Old Guy in Space
TIME
Reader's Digest
THE WALL STREET JOURNAL
Snooty Stock Market Publication Too Cheap to Run Comics
Buy High, Panic Later
© DAN PIRARO · 1999

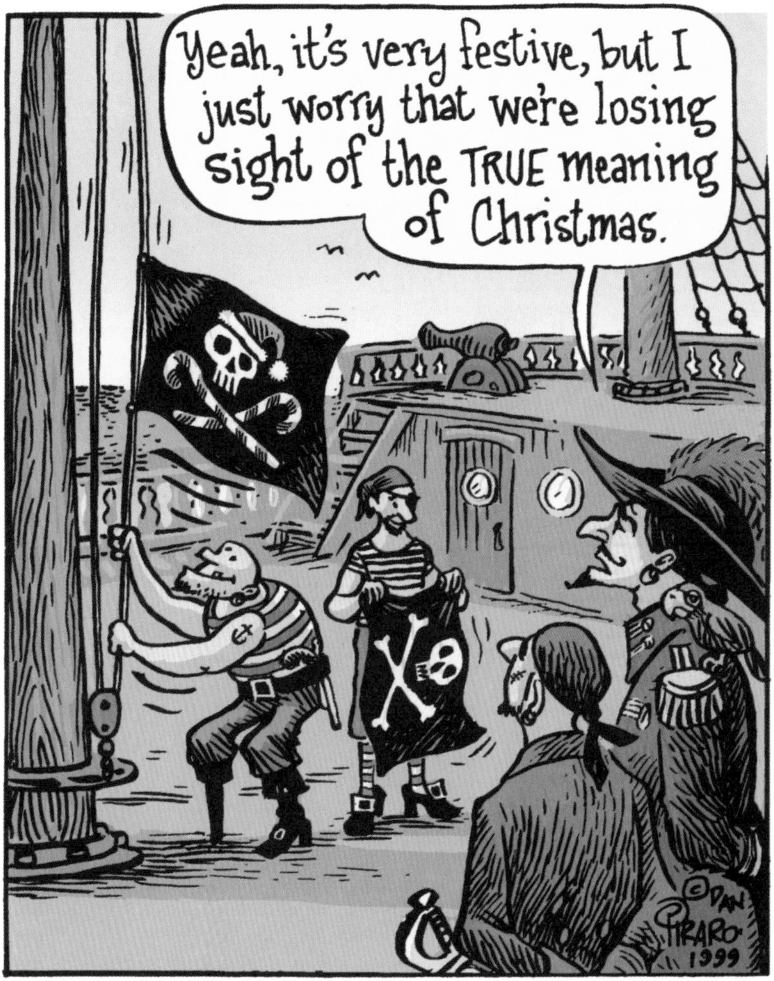
Yeah, it's very festive, but I just worry that we're losing sight of the TRUE meaning of Christmas.
©DAN PIRARO 1999

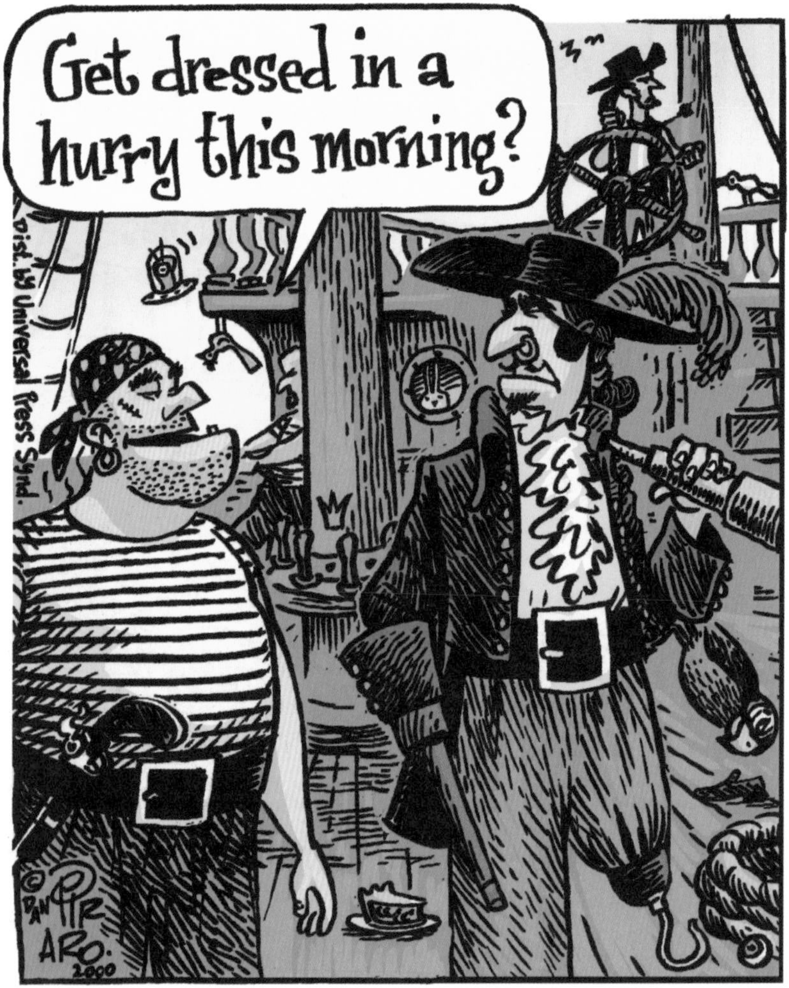
Get dressed in a hurry this morning?
Dist. by Universal Press Synd.
© DAN PIRARO. 2000

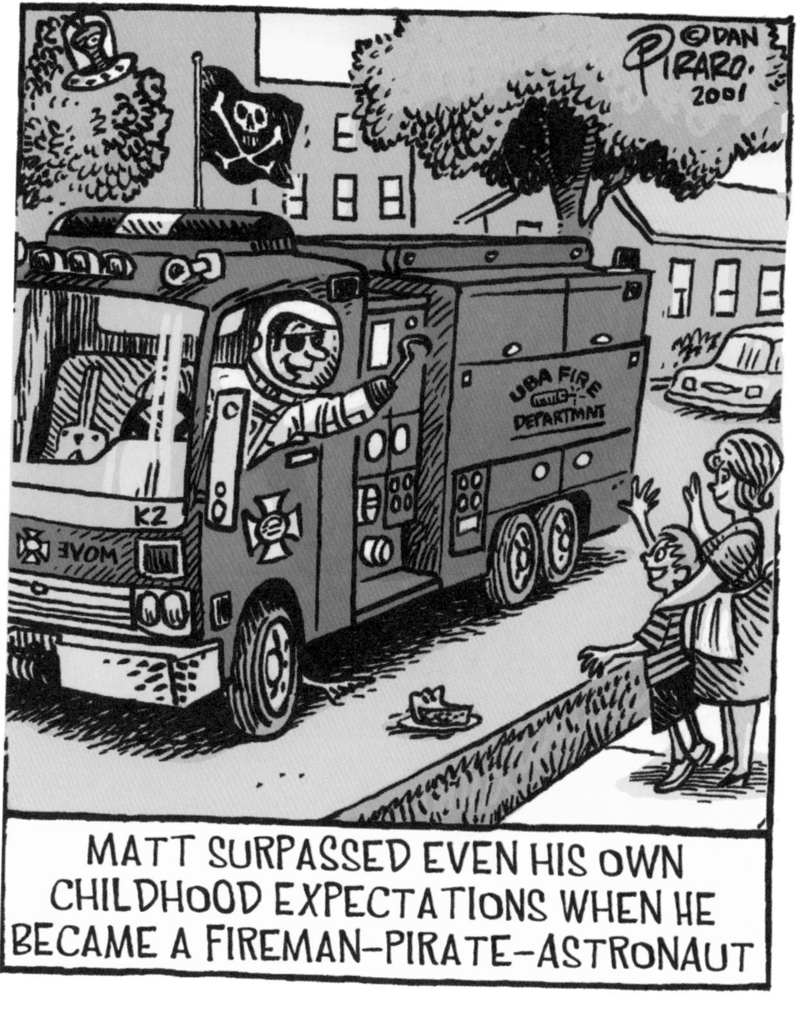
© DAN PIRARO. 2001
UBA FIRE DEPARTMNT
K2

MATT SURPASSED EVEN HIS OWN CHILDHOOD EXPECTATIONS WHEN HE BECAME A FIREMAN-PIRATE-ASTRONAUT

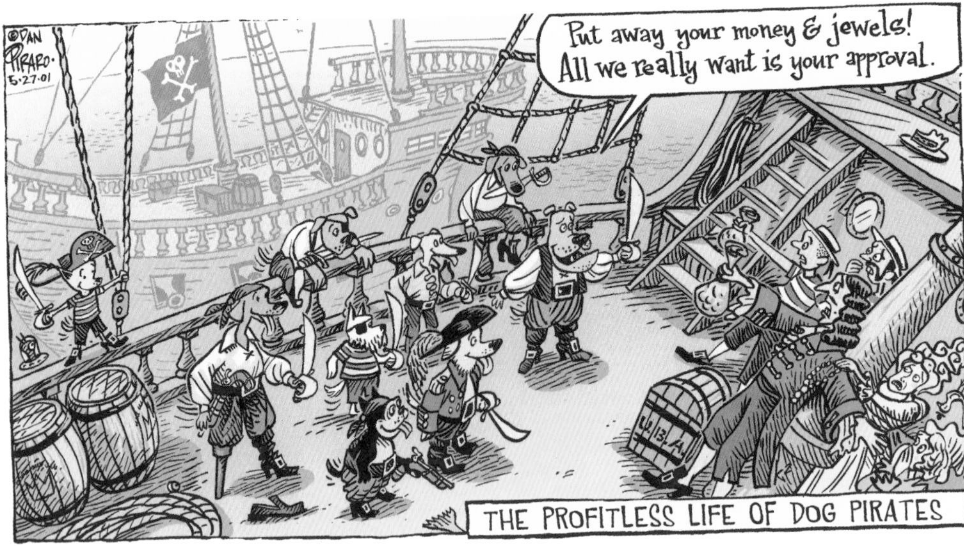
©DAN PIRARO 5·27·01
Put away your money & jewels! All we really want is your approval.
THE PROFITLESS LIFE OF DOG PIRATES

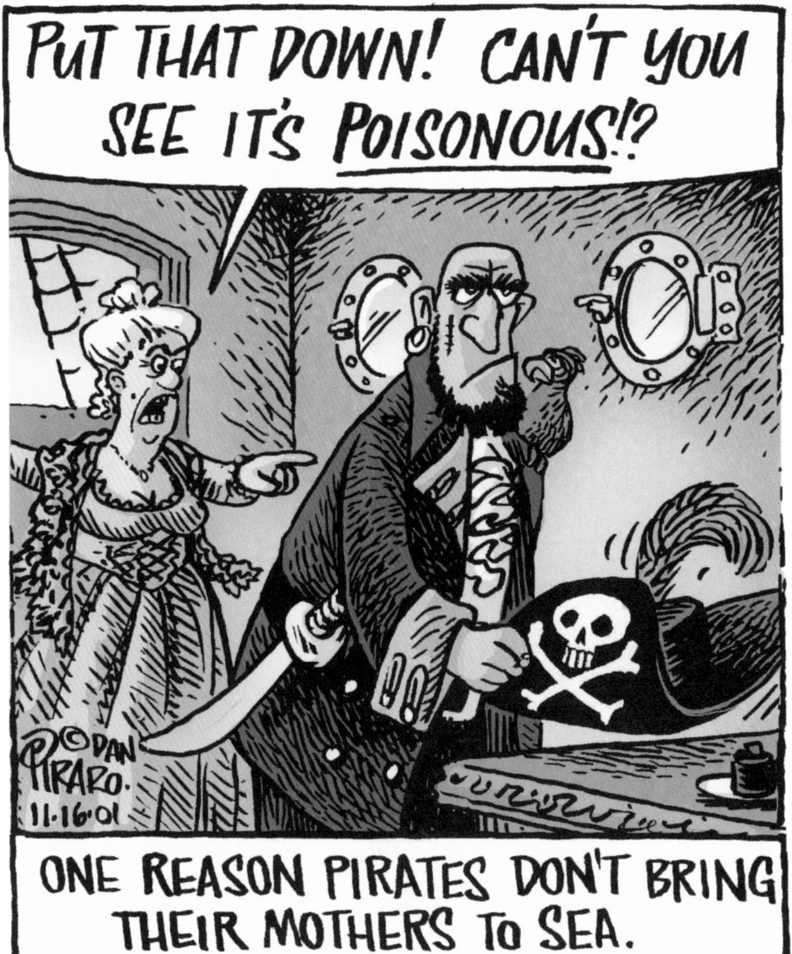
PUT THAT DOWN! CAN'T YOU SEE IT'S POISONOUS!?
© DAN PIRARO 11·16·01
ONE REASON PIRATES DON'T BRING THEIR MOTHERS TO SEA.

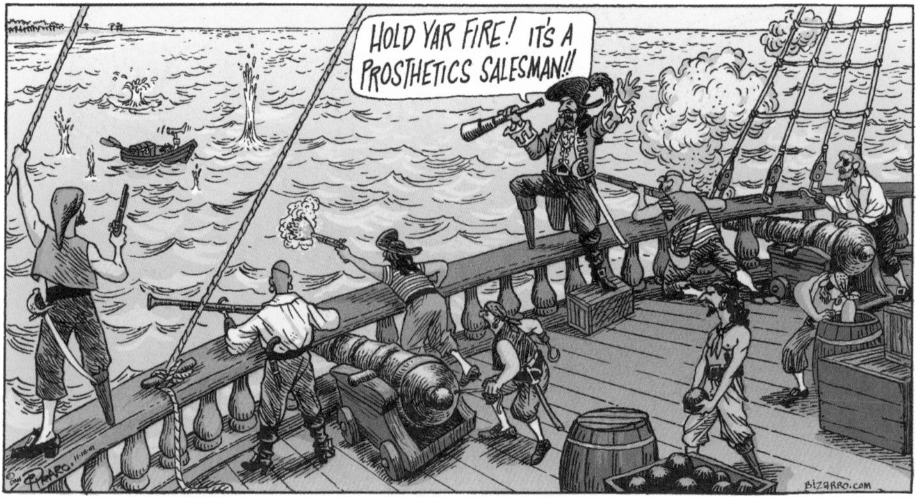
HOLD YAR FIRE! IT'S A PROSTHETICS SALESMAN!!
BIZARRO.COM

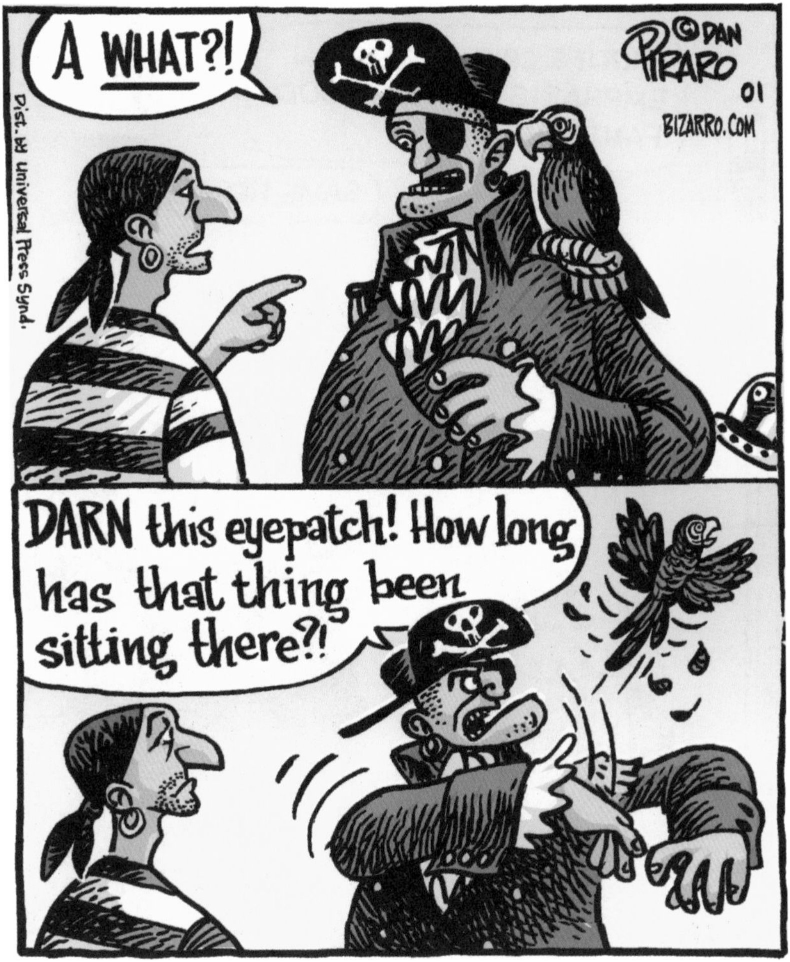
A WHAT?!
© DAN PIRARO 01
BIZARRO.COM
Dist. by Universal Press Synd.
DARN this eyepatch! How long has that thing been sitting there?!

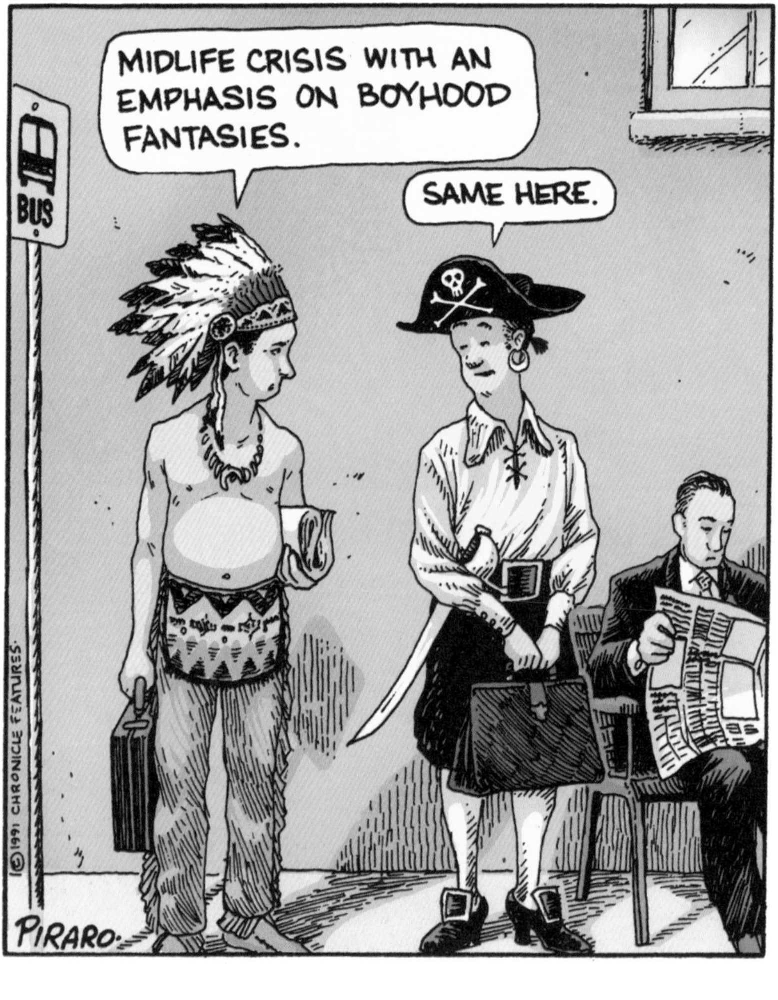
MIDLIFE CRISIS WITH AN EMPHASIS ON BOYHOOD FANTASIES.
SAME HERE.
BUS
©1991 CHRONICLE FEATURES.
PIRARO

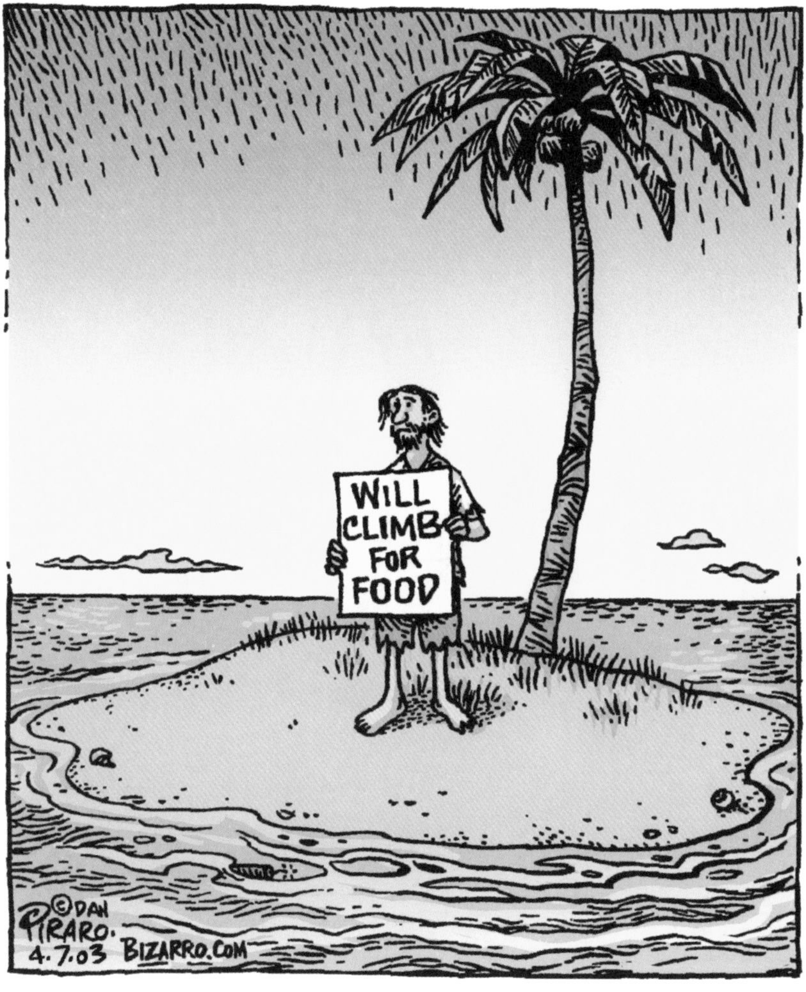
WILL CLIMB FOR FOOD
©DAN PIRARO. 4.7.03 BIZARRO.COM

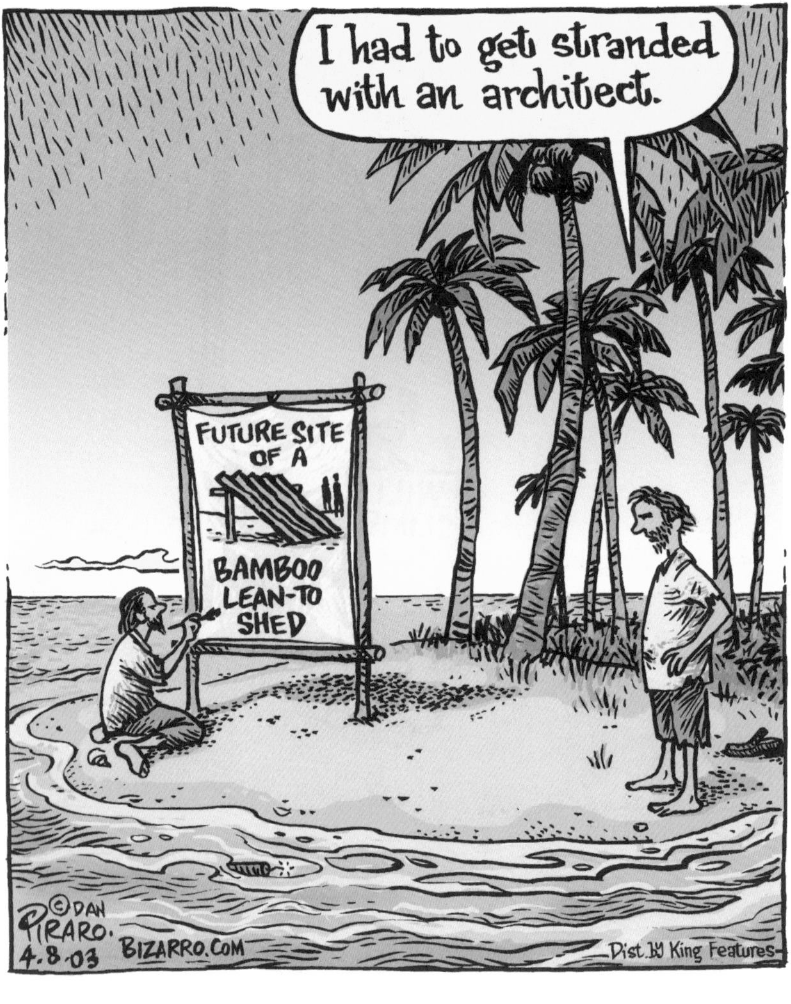
I had to get stranded with an architect.
FUTURE SITE OF A BAMBOO LEAN-TO SHED
© DAN PIRARO. 4.8.03
BIZARRO.COM
Dist. by King Features

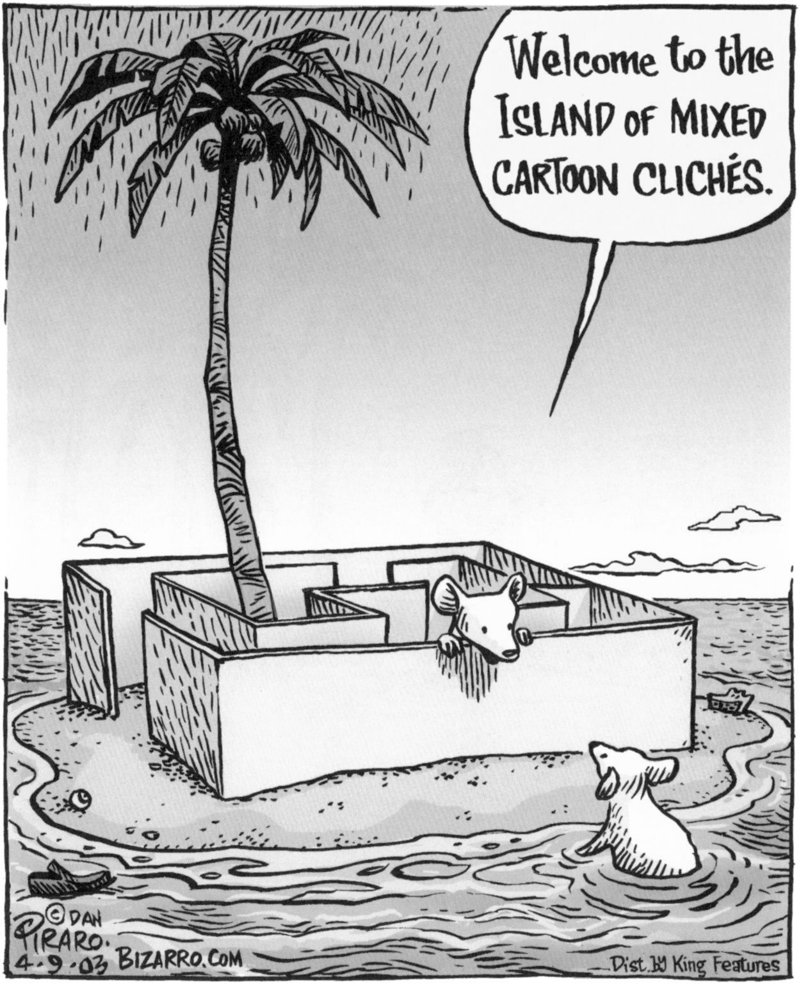

Welcome to the ISLAND OF MIXED CARTOON CLICHÉS.
© DAN PIRARO. 4-9-03 BIZARRO.COM
Dist. by King Features

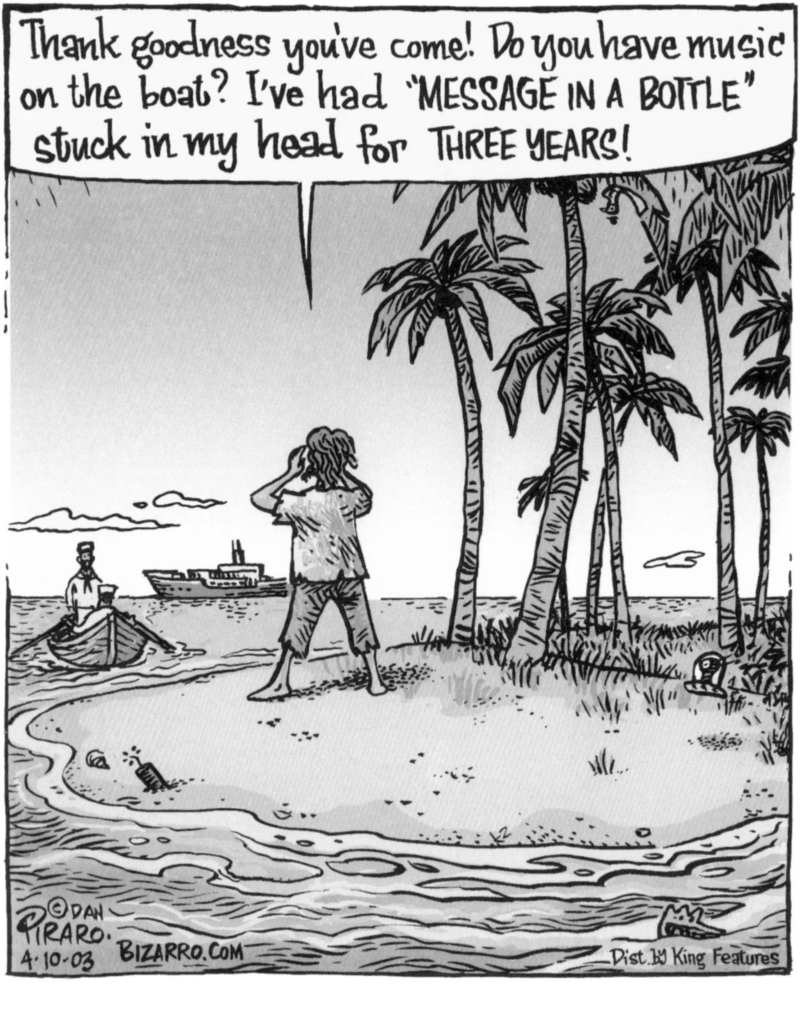
Thank goodness you've come! Do you have music on the boat? I've had "MESSAGE IN A BOTTLE" stuck in my head for THREE YEARS!
©DAN PIRARO. 4-10-03
BIZARRO.COM
Dist. by King Features

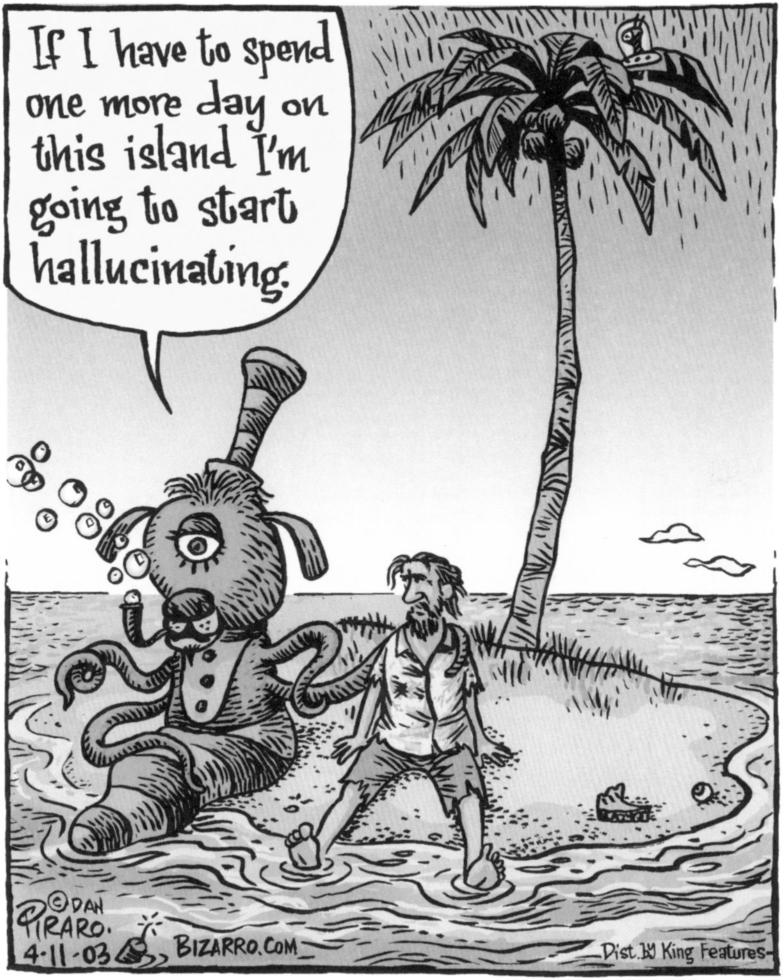
If I have to spend one more day on this island I'm going to start hallucinating.
©DAN PIRARO. 4-11-03
BIZARRO.COM
Dist. by King Features

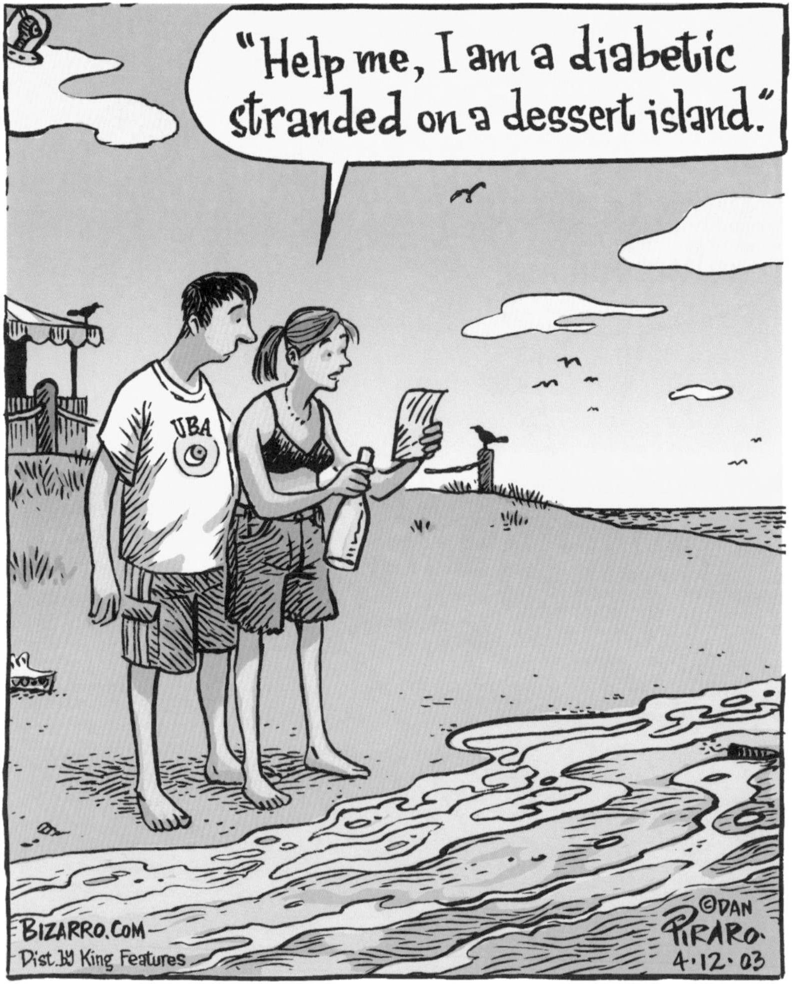
"Help me, I am a diabetic stranded on a dessert island."
UBA
BIZARRO.COM
Dist. by King Features
©DAN PIRARO 4·12·03

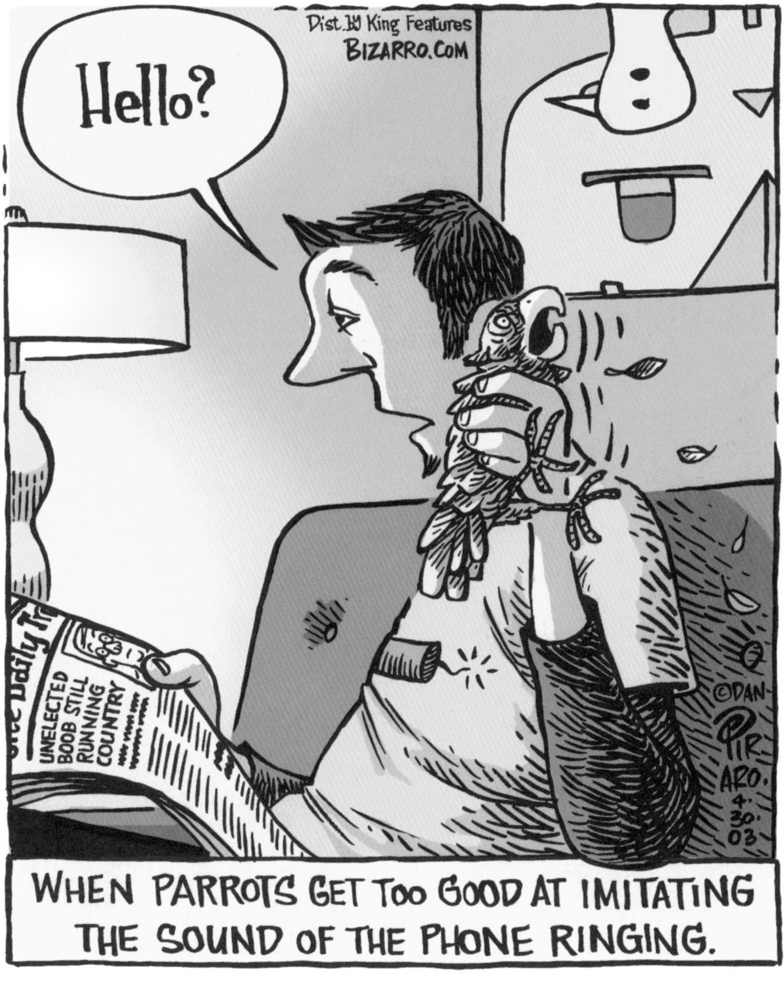
Hello?
Dist. by King Features
BIZARRO.COM
UNELECTED BOOB STILL RUNNING COUNTRY
©DAN-PIRARO. 4.30.03

WHEN PARROTS GET TOO GOOD AT IMITATING THE SOUND OF THE PHONE RINGING.

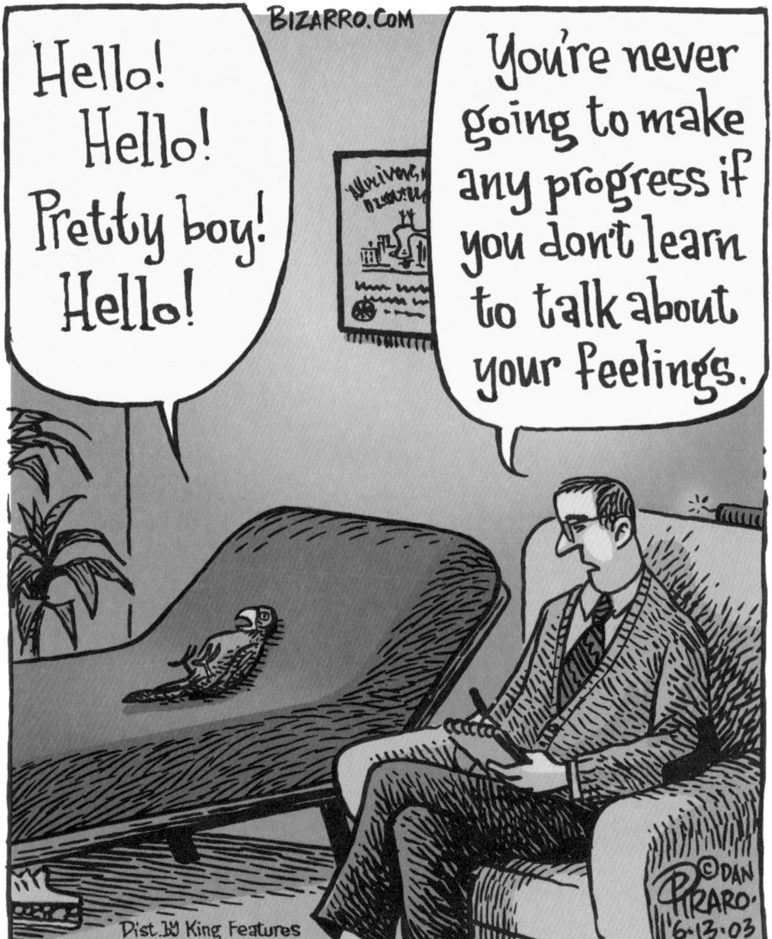
BIZARRO.COM
Hello! Hello! Pretty boy! Hello!
You're never going to make any progress if you don't learn to talk about your feelings.
Dist. by King Features
©DAN PIRARO 6-13-03

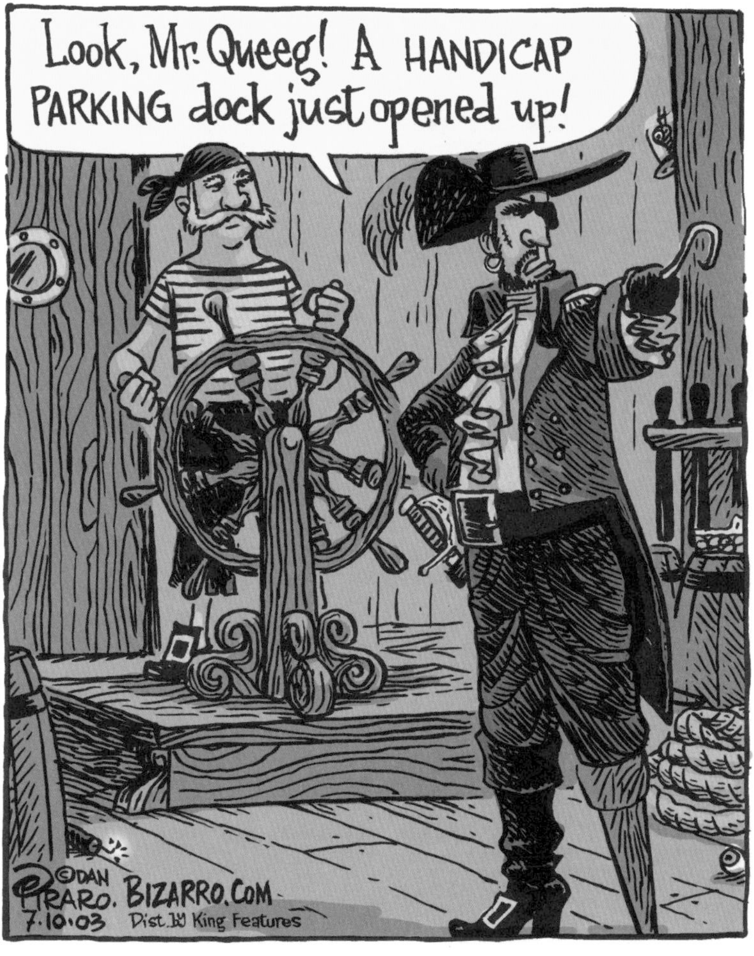
Look, Mr. Queeg! A HANDICAP PARKING dock just opened up!
©DAN PIRARO. BIZARRO.COM
7.10.03 Dist. by King Features

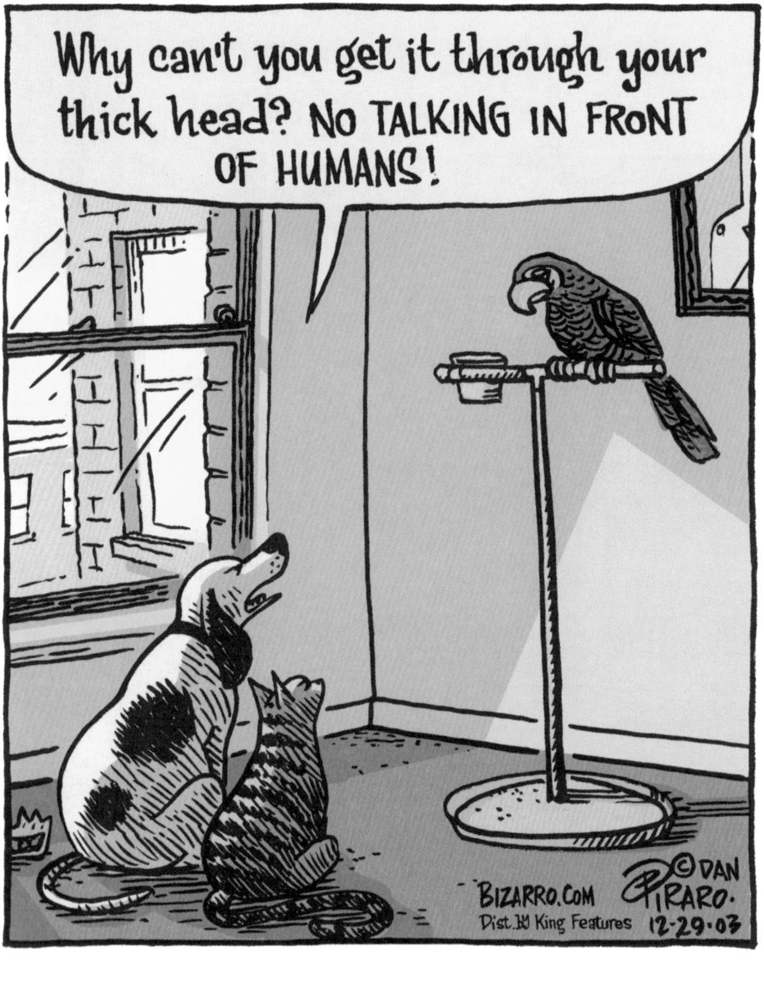
Why can't you get it through your thick head? NO TALKING IN FRONT OF HUMANS!
BIZARRO.COM
Dist. by King Features
© DAN PIRARO. 12-29-03

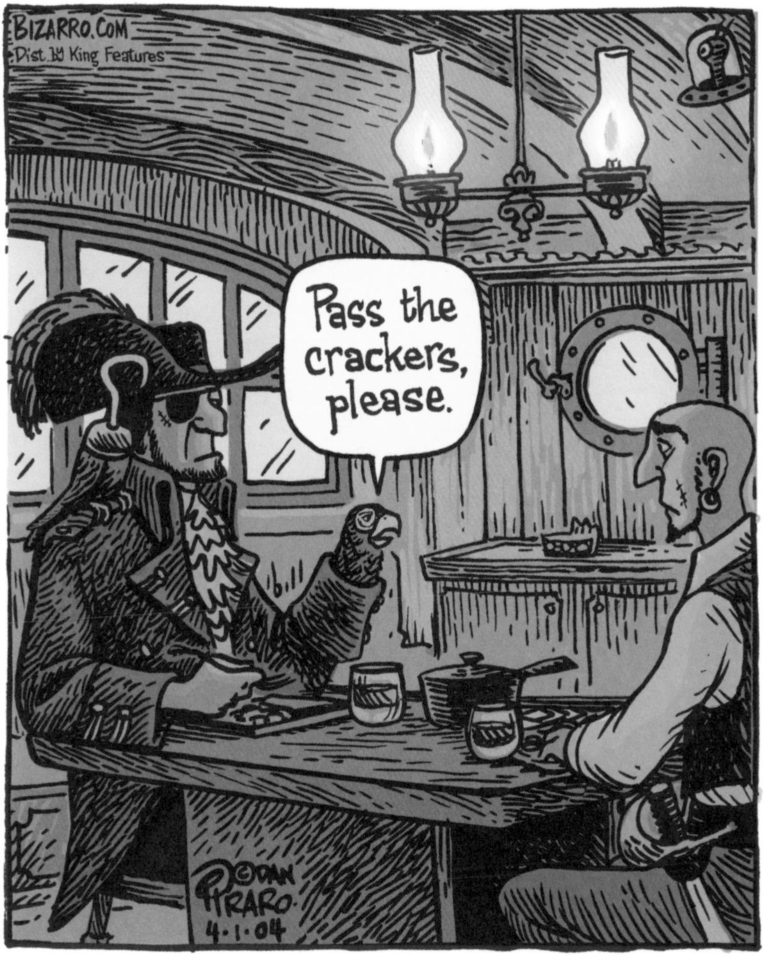
BIZARRO.COM
Dist. by King Features
Pass the crackers, please.
©DAN PIRARO 4·1·04

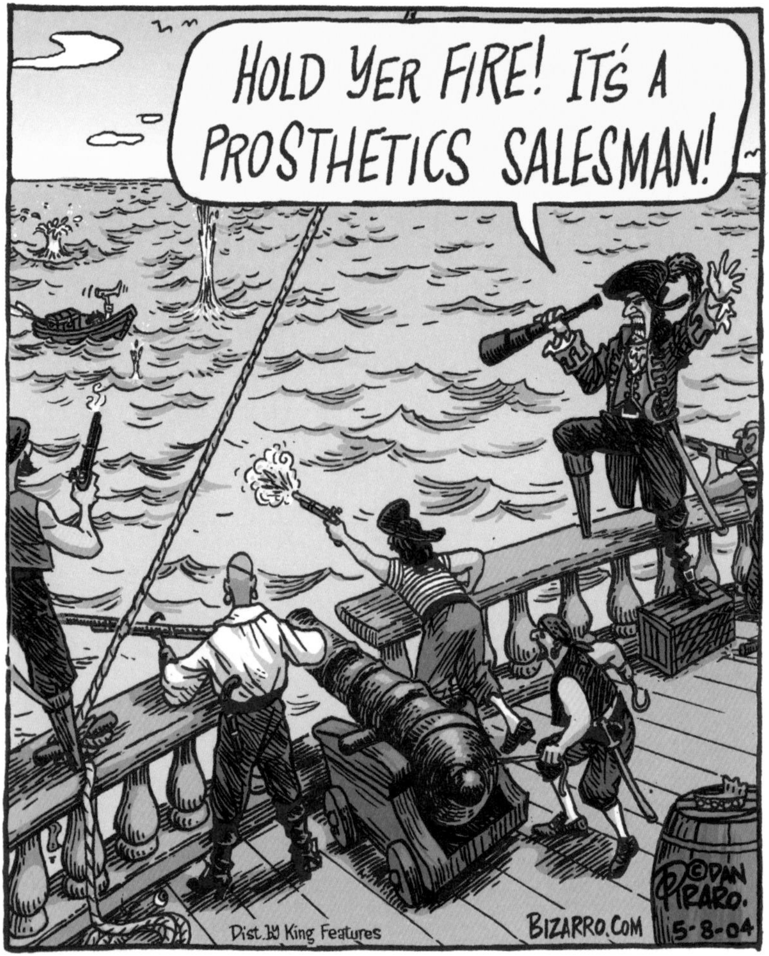
HOLD YER FIRE! IT'S A PROSTHETICS SALESMAN!
Dist. by King Features
BIZARRO.COM
©DAN PIRARO. 5-8-04

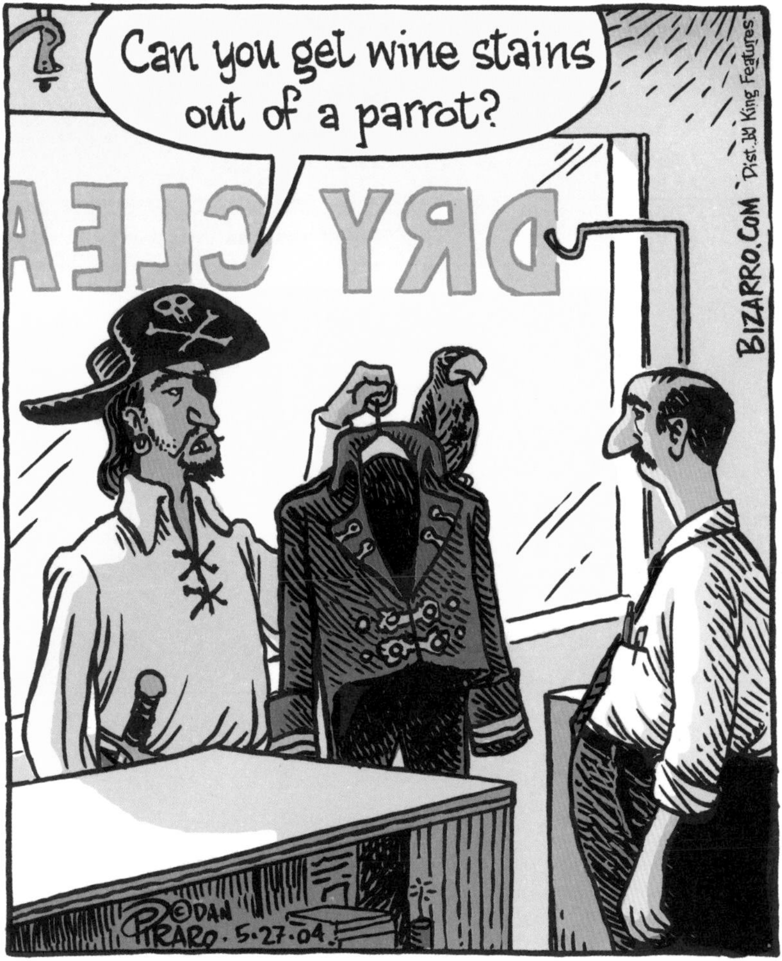
Can you get wine stains out of a parrot?
BIZARRO.COM Dist. by King Features
©DAN PIRARO 5-27-04

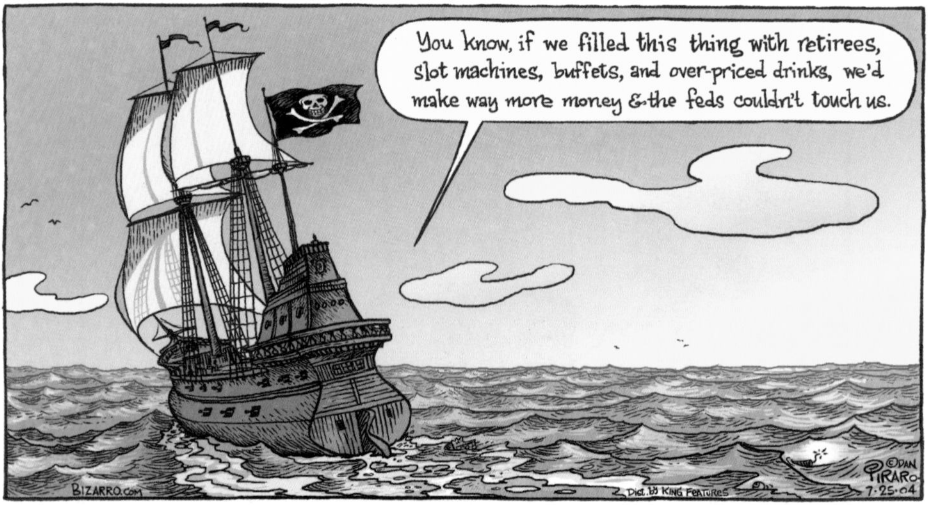
You know, if we filled this thing with retirees, slot machines, buffets, and over-priced drinks, we'd make way more money & the feds couldn't touch us.
BIZARRO.COM
Dist. by KING FEATURES
©DAN PIRARO 7.25.04

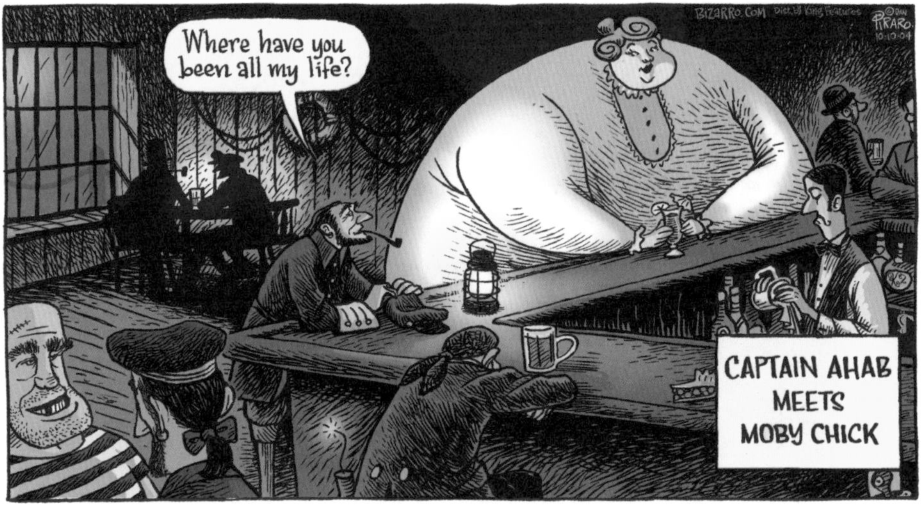

BIZARRO.COM
PIRARO.
10-10-04
Where have you been all my life?
CAPTAIN AHAB MEETS MOBY CHICK

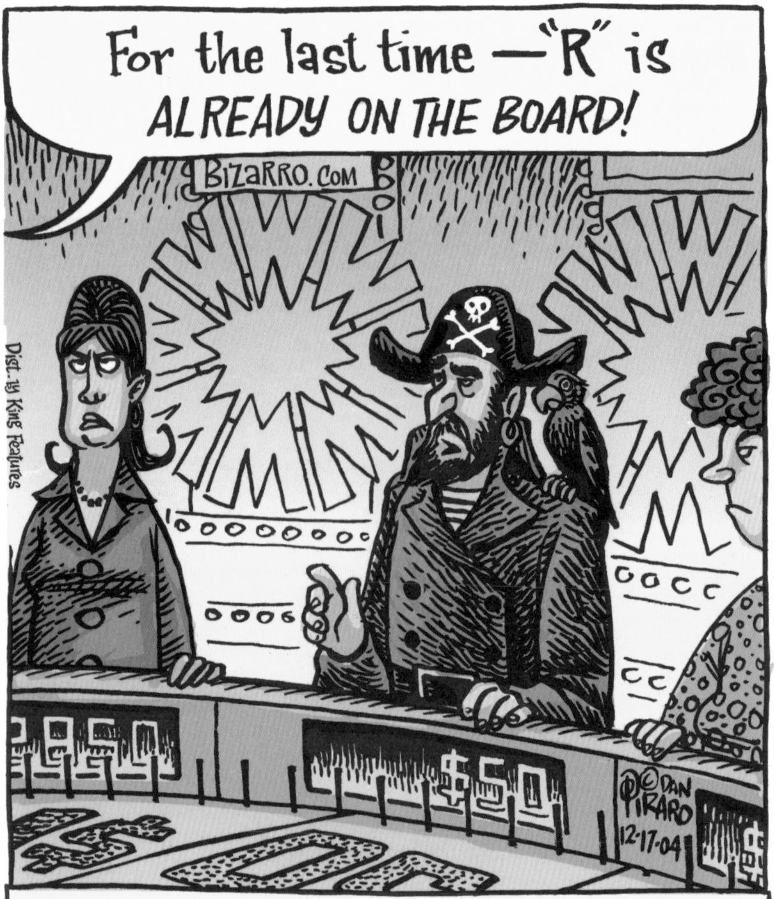
For the last time — "R" is ALREADY ON THE BOARD!
BIZARRO.COM
Dist. by King Features
$50
©DAN PIRARO 12-17-04

LONG JOHN SILVER on WHEEL OF FORTUNE

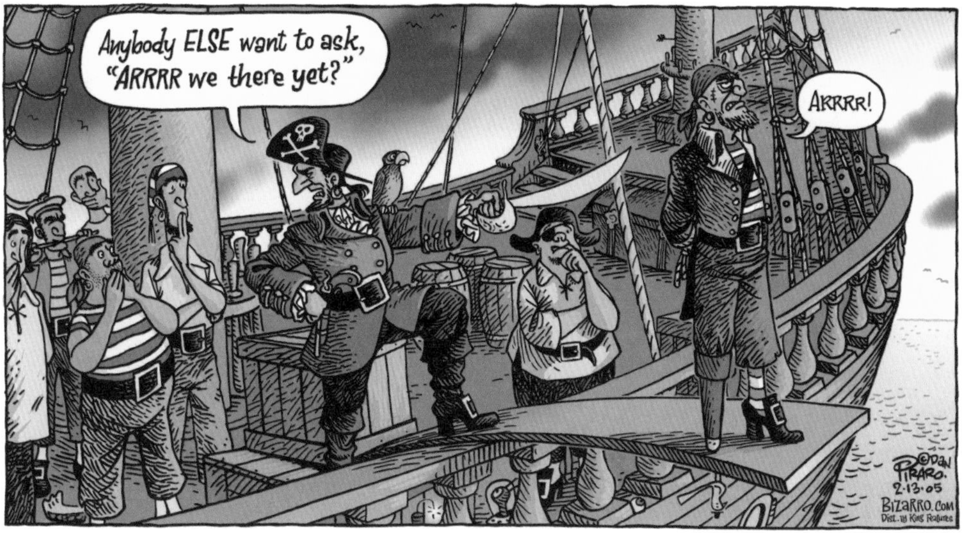
Anybody ELSE want to ask, "ARRRR we there yet?"
ARRRR!
©DAN PIRARO 2·13·05
BIZARRO.COM
Dist. by King Features

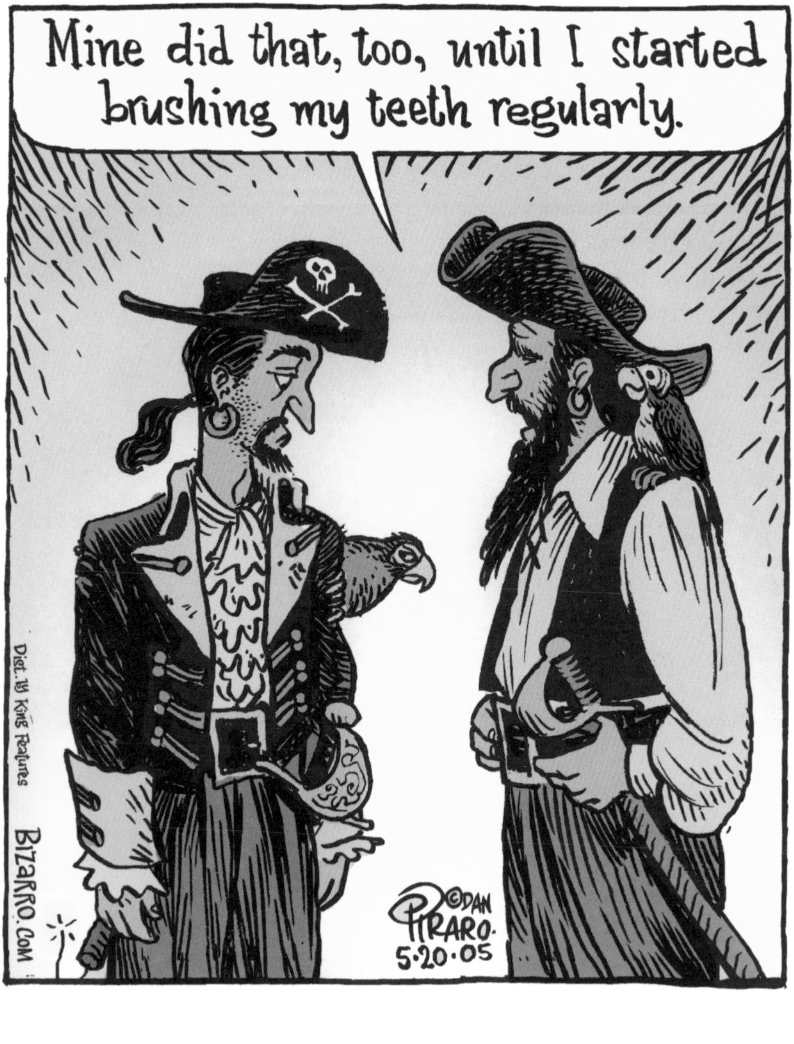
Mine did that, too, until I started brushing my teeth regularly.
Dist. by King Features
BIZARRO.COM
©DAN PIRARO 5·20·05

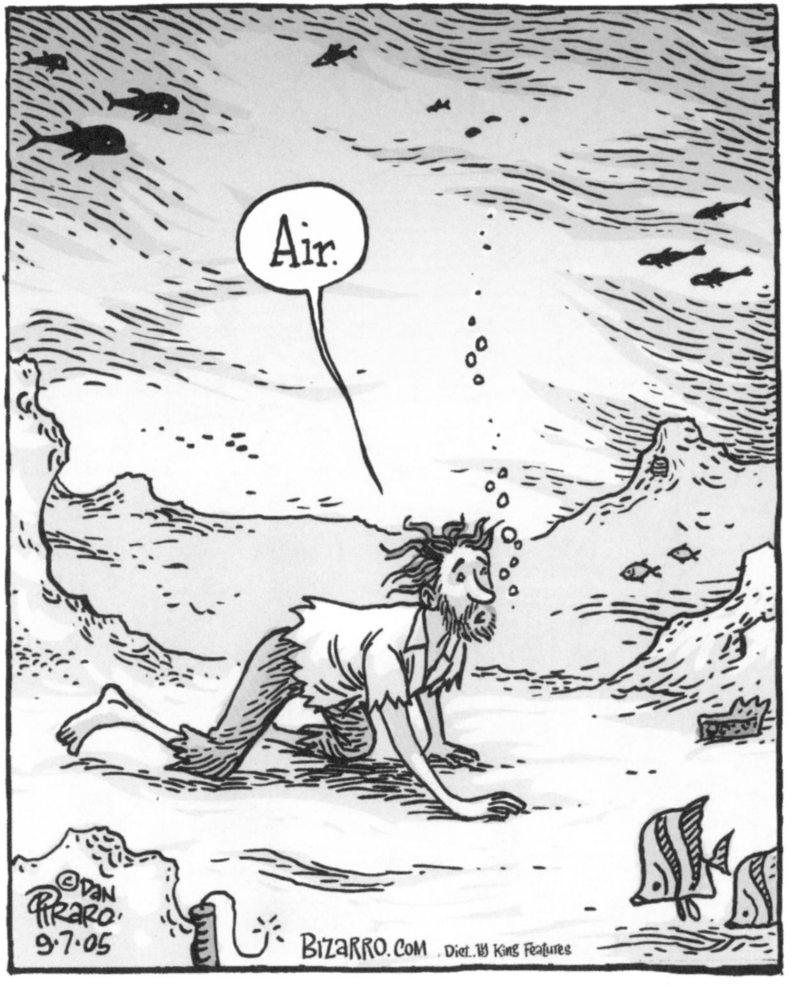
Air.
©DAN PIRARO 9·7·05
BIZARRO.COM
Dist. by King Features

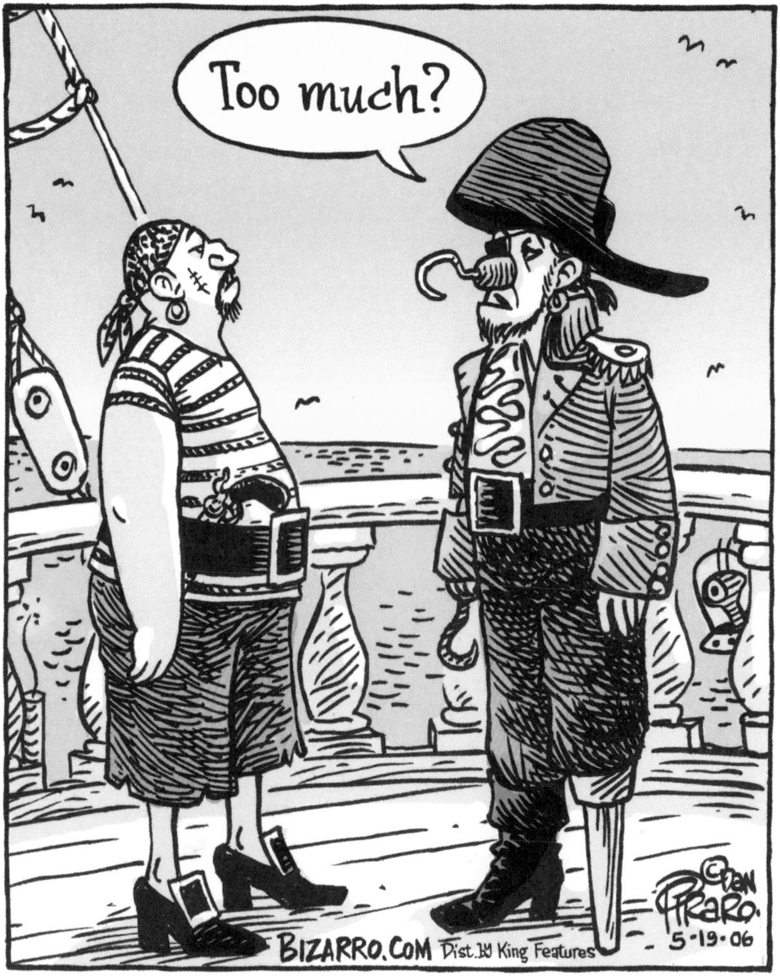
Too much?
BIZARRO.COM Dist. by King Features
©Dan Piraro. 5-19-06

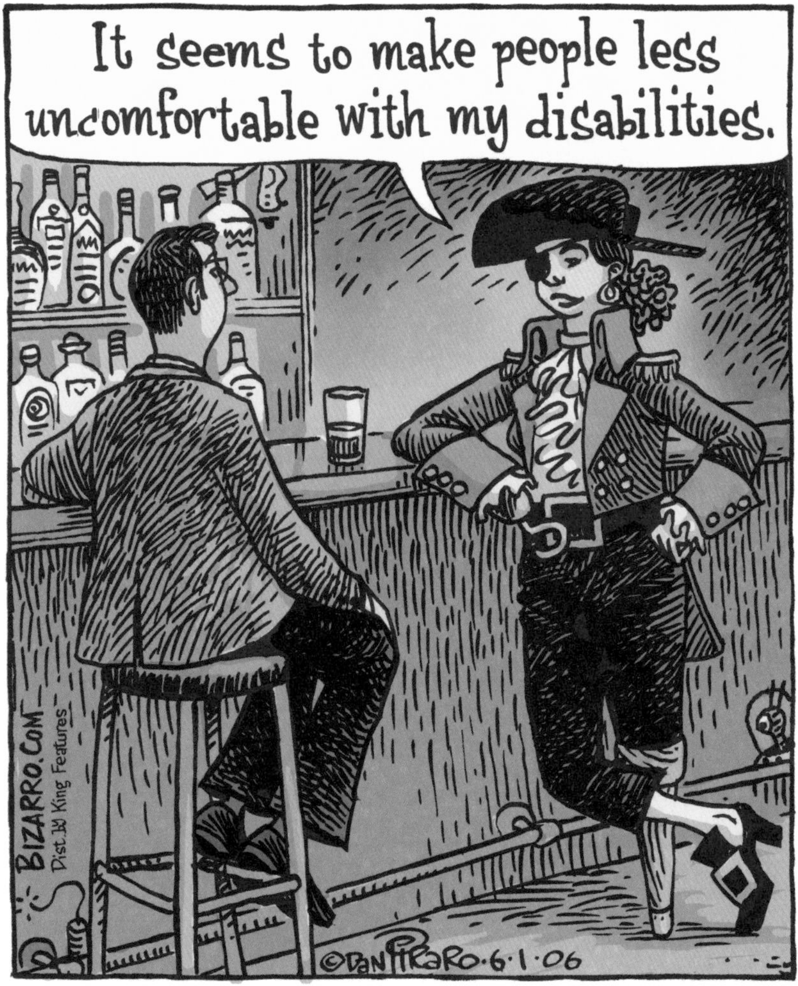
It seems to make people less uncomfortable with my disabilities.
BIZARRO.COM
Dist. by King Features
©DAN PIRARO·6·1·06

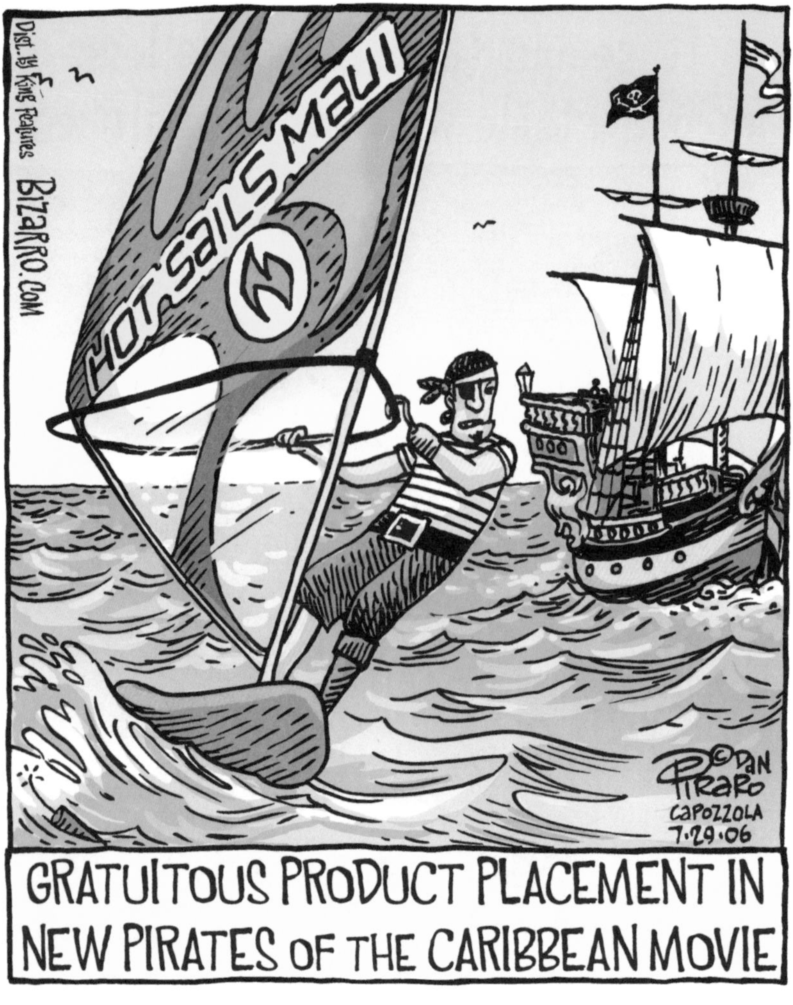
HOT SAILS MAUI
Dist. by King Features
BIZARRO.COM
© DAN PIRARO
CAPOZZOLA
7·29·06

GRATUITOUS PRODUCT PLACEMENT IN NEW PIRATES OF THE CARIBBEAN MOVIE

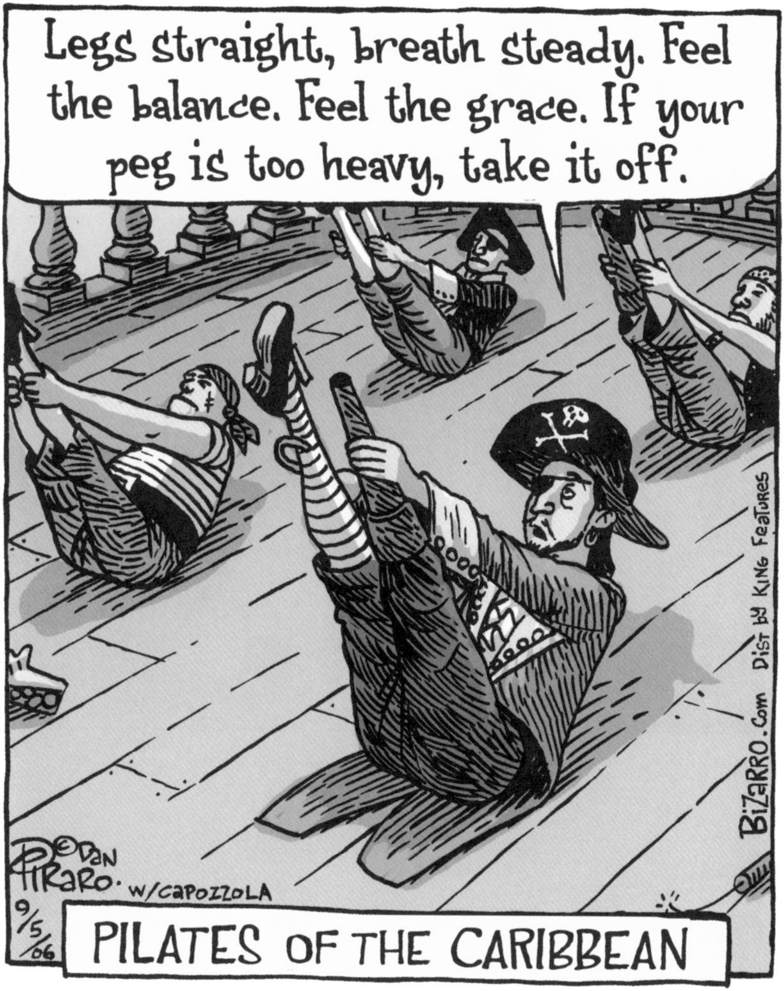
Legs straight, breath steady. Feel the balance. Feel the grace. If your peg is too heavy, take it off.
©DAN PIRARO. W/CAPOZZOLA
9/5/06
BIZARRO.Com DIST BY KING FEATURES
PILATES OF THE CARIBBEAN

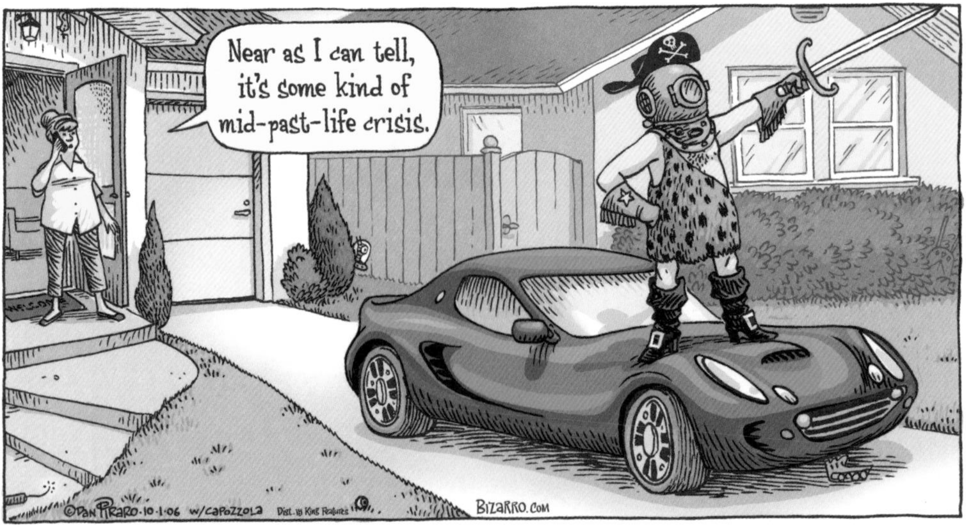
Near as I can tell, it's some kind of mid-past-life crisis.
©DAN PIRARO·10·1·06 w/CAPOZZOLA
Dist. by King Features
BIZARRO.COM

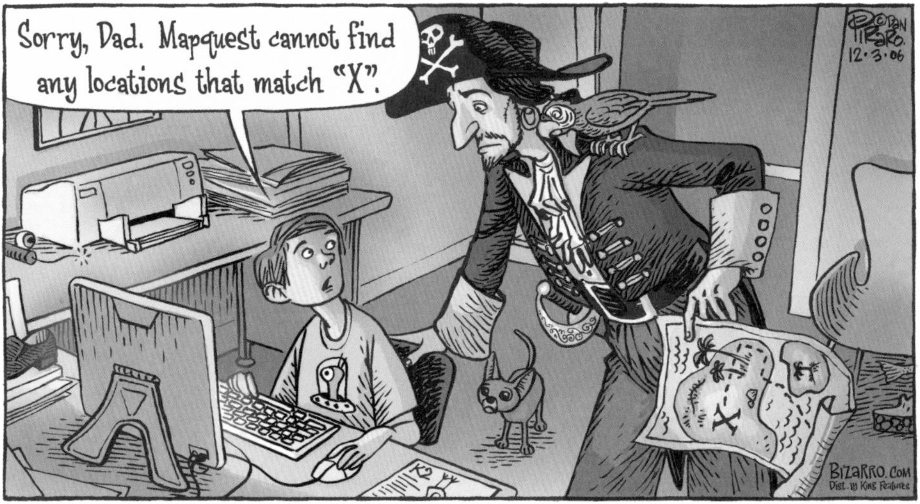
Sorry, Dad. Mapquest cannot find any locations that match "X".
DAN PIRARO 12·3·06
BIZARRO.COM
Dist. by King Features

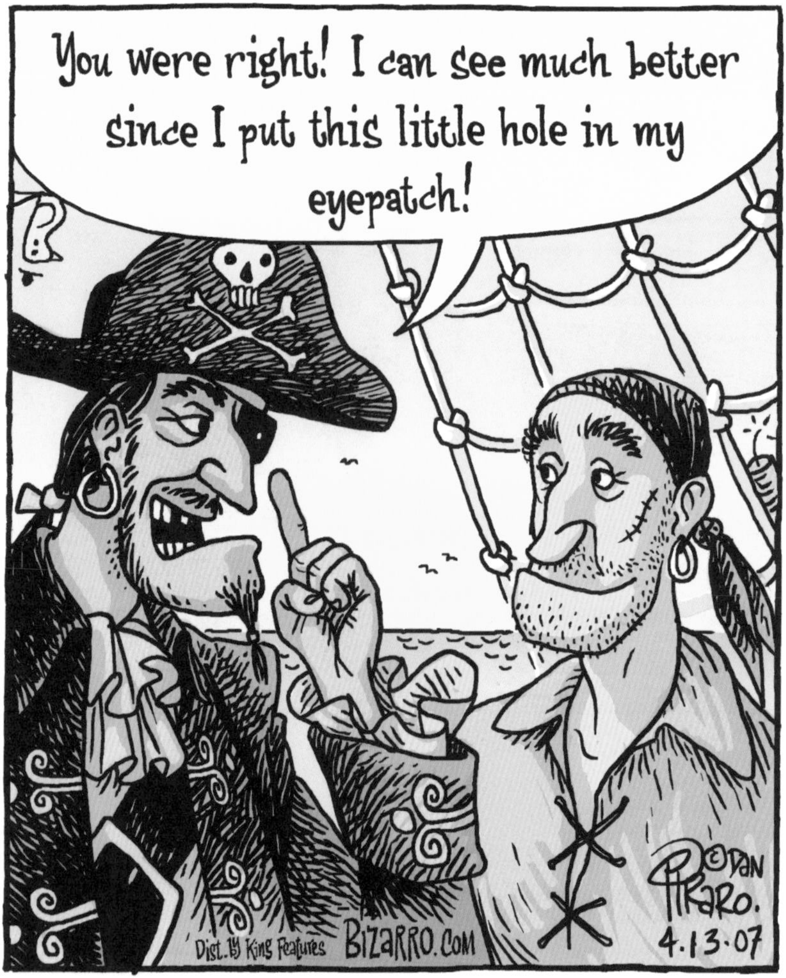
You were right! I can see much better since I put this little hole in my eyepatch!
Dist. by King Features
BIZARRO.COM
©DAN PIRARO. 4.13.07

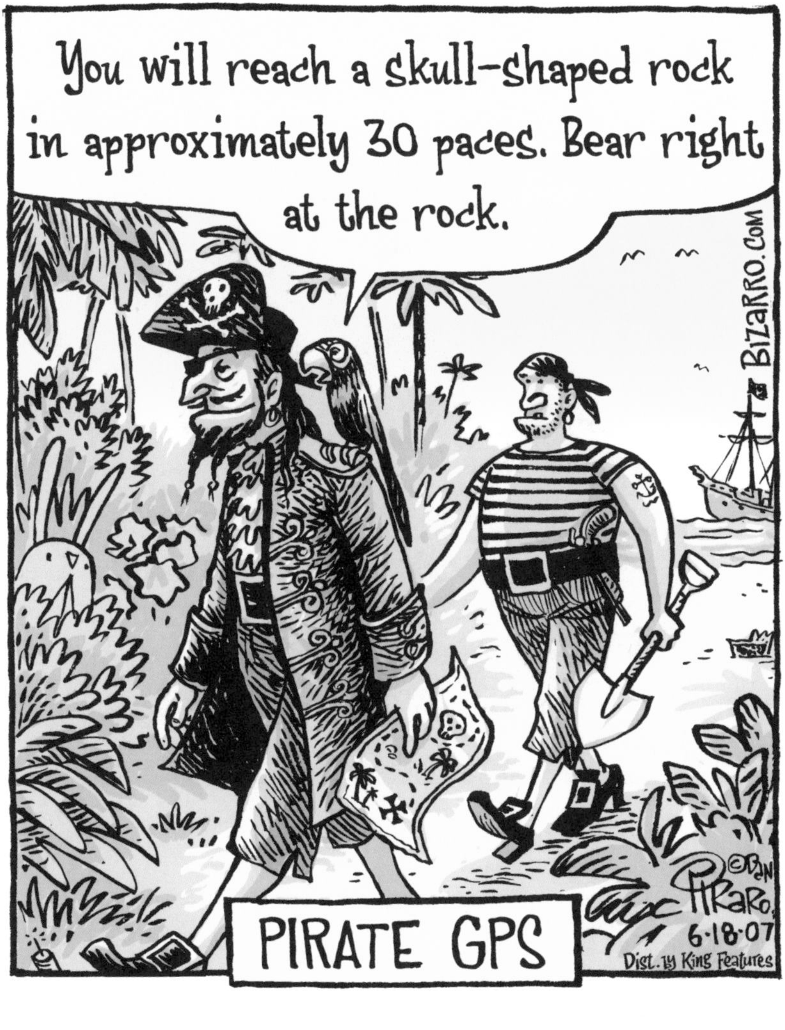
You will reach a skull-shaped rock in approximately 30 paces. Bear right at the rock.
BIZARRO.COM
PIRATE GPS
© Dan Piraro 6-18-07
Dist. by King Features

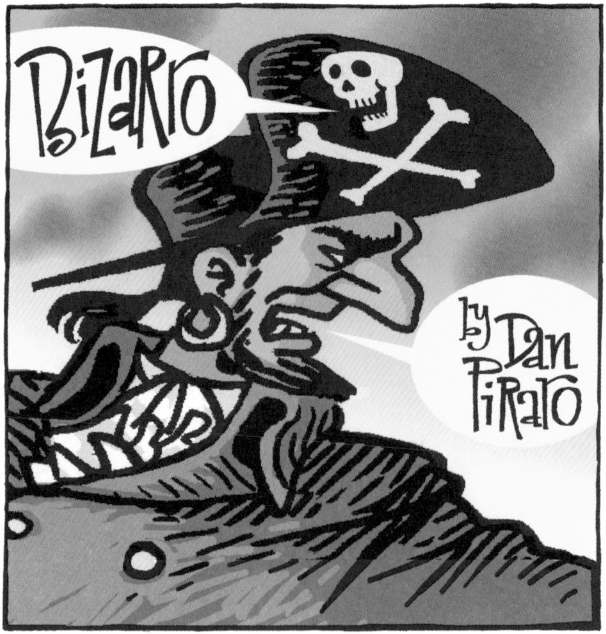
Bizarro
by Dan Piraro

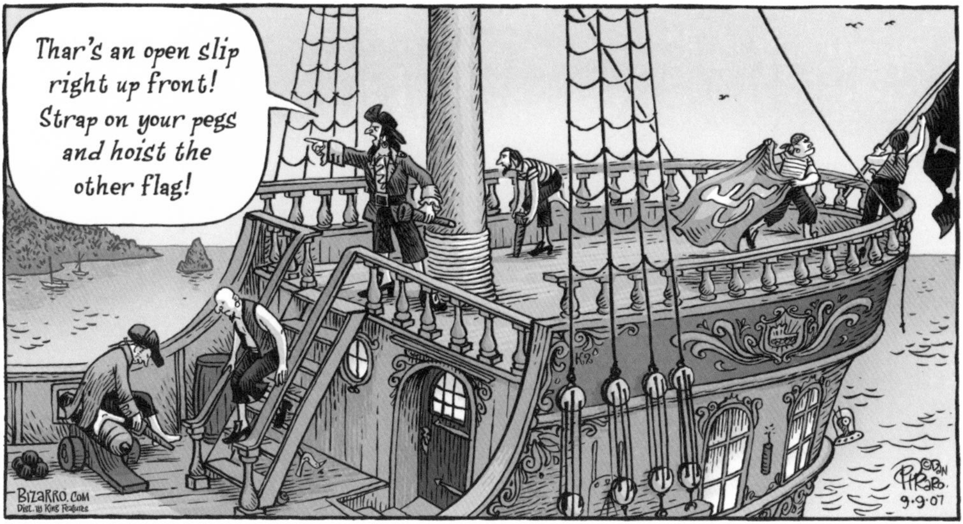
Thar's an open slip right up front! Strap on your pegs and hoist the other flag!
BIZARRO.COM
Dist. by King Features
©Dan Piraro 9·9·07

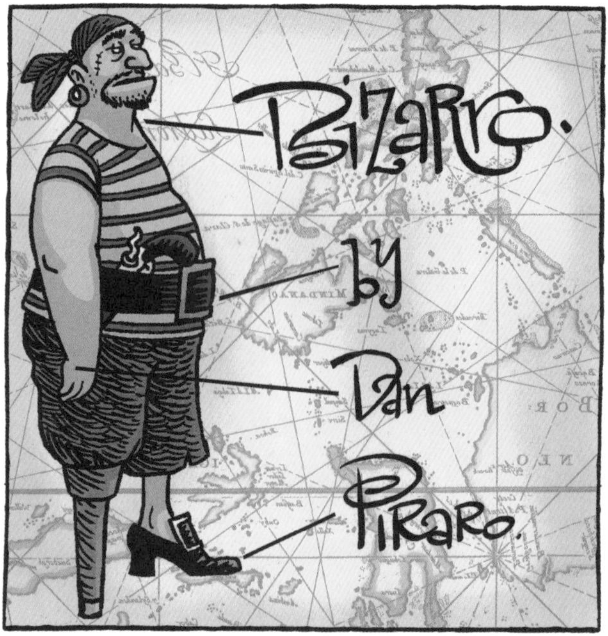
Bizarro.
by
Dan
Piraro.

Pirates Illustrated

EYE PATCH
Looks cool.
Switches eyes
regularly to
avoid head-
aches.

**SKULL & CROSS-
BONES ON HAT**
Pirate hats
are poisonous.
If you eat one,
you could die.

**RUFFLY
SHIRT**
Pirates
were in-
famous
for not
return-
ing
entire
tuxedo.

PARROT
Original
choice
of Golden
Retrievers
caused
bursitis.

**HOOK
HAND**
Far more
versatile
than a
ball peen
hand.

PEG LEG
Named for
Peggy Jackson,
known for
using a fake
one so she could park
in handicap spaces.

**GIANT BUCKLE
ON SHOE**
Who doesn't
like a
little bling?

BIZARRO.COM
Dist. by King Features
©DAN PIRARO · 10·7·07

71

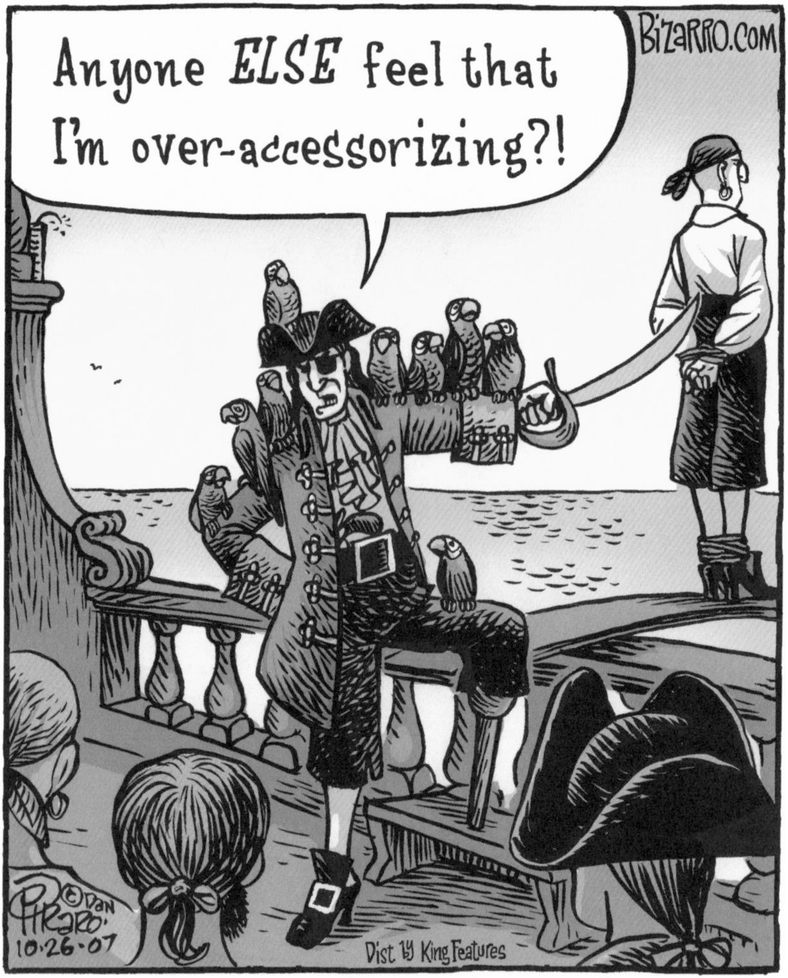
Anyone ELSE feel that I'm over-accessorizing?!
BIZARRO.COM
©DAN PIRARO 10-26-07
Dist. by King Features

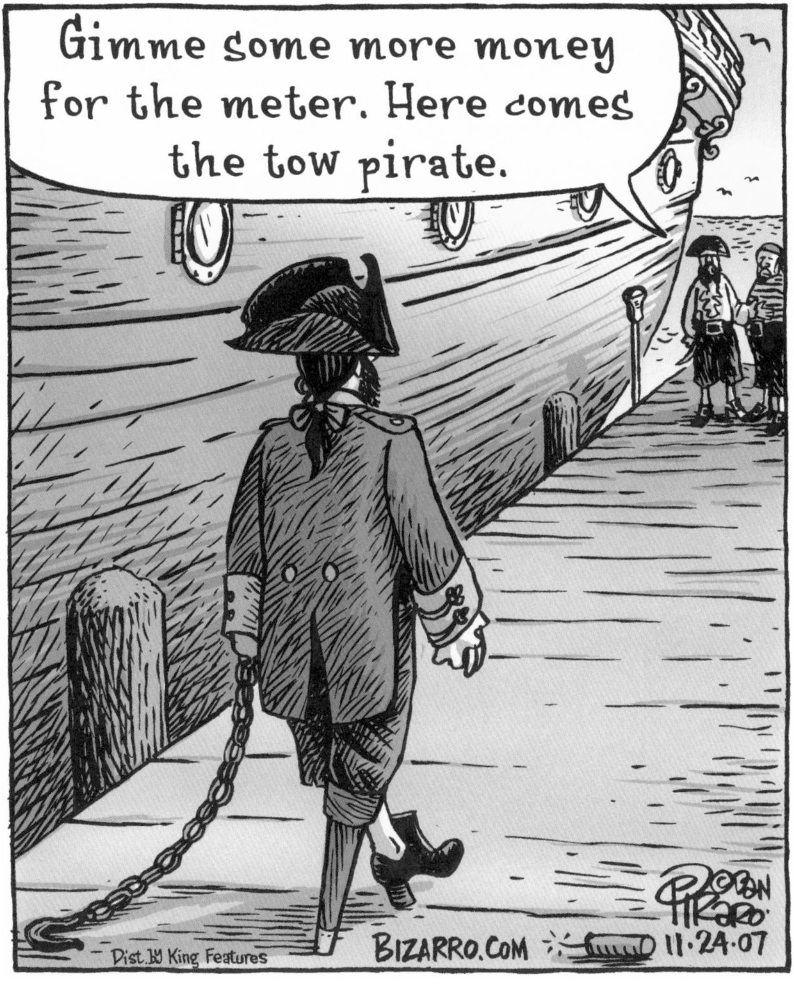
Gimme some more money for the meter. Here comes the tow pirate.
Dist. by King Features
BIZARRO.COM
11·24·07

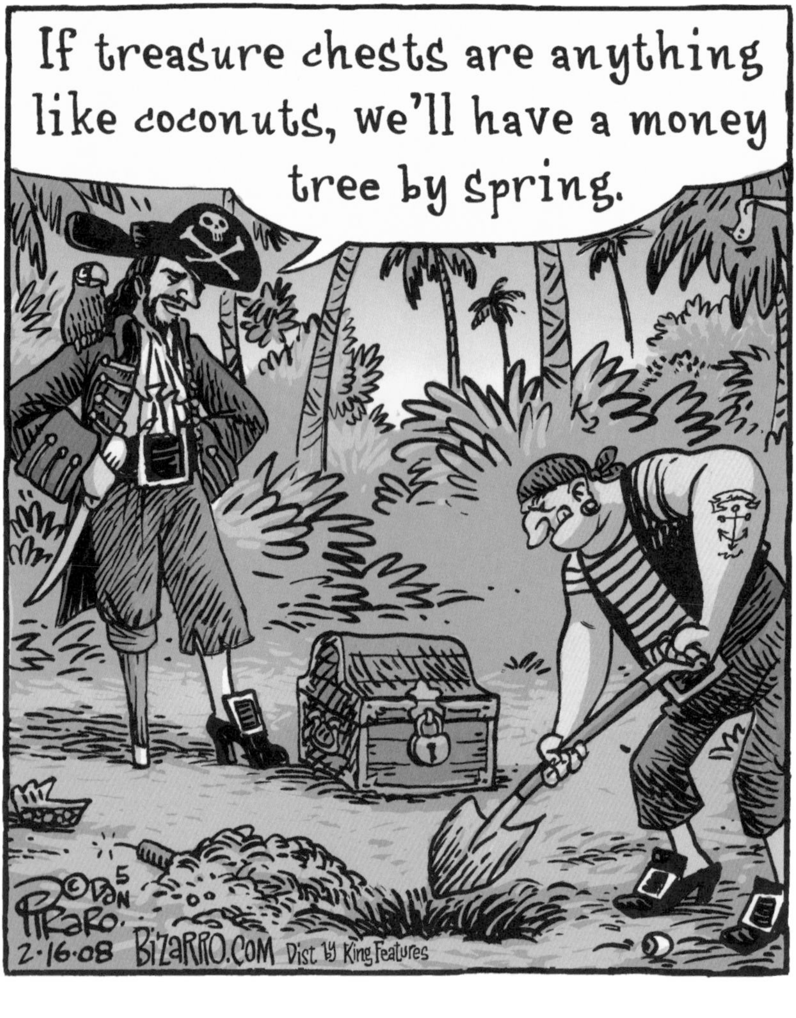

If treasure chests are anything like coconuts, we'll have a money tree by Spring.
©Dan Piraro 2-16-08 BiZARRO.COM Dist. by King Features

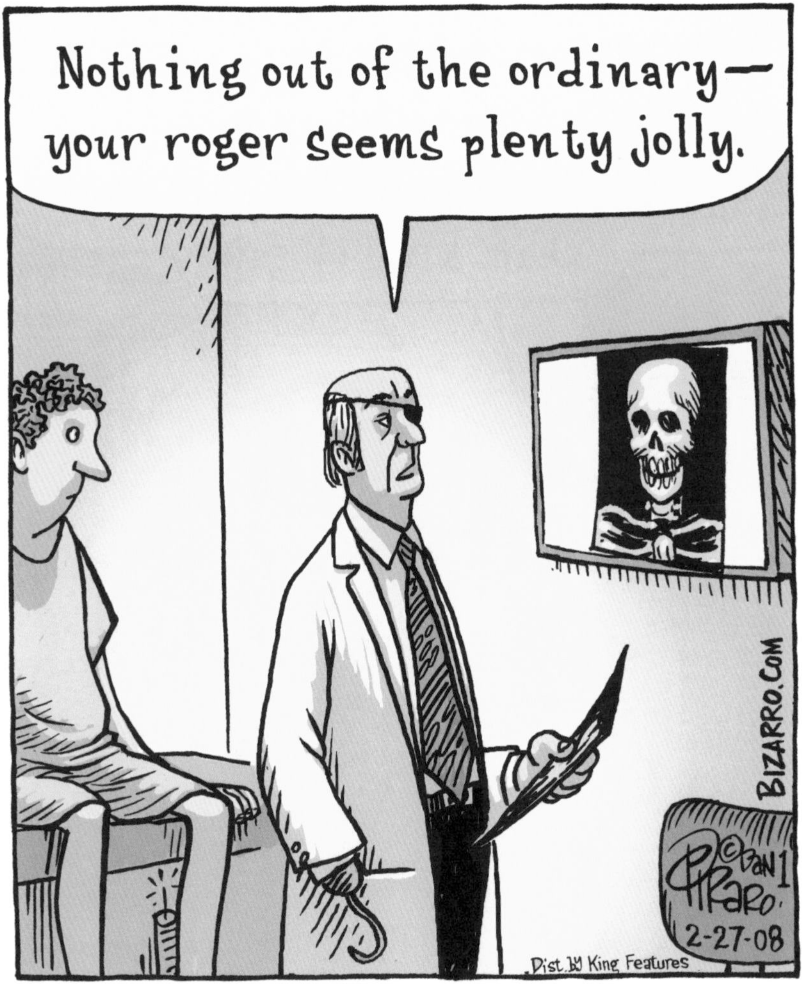
Nothing out of the ordinary—
your roger seems plenty jolly.
BIZARRO.COM
2-27-08
Dist. by King Features

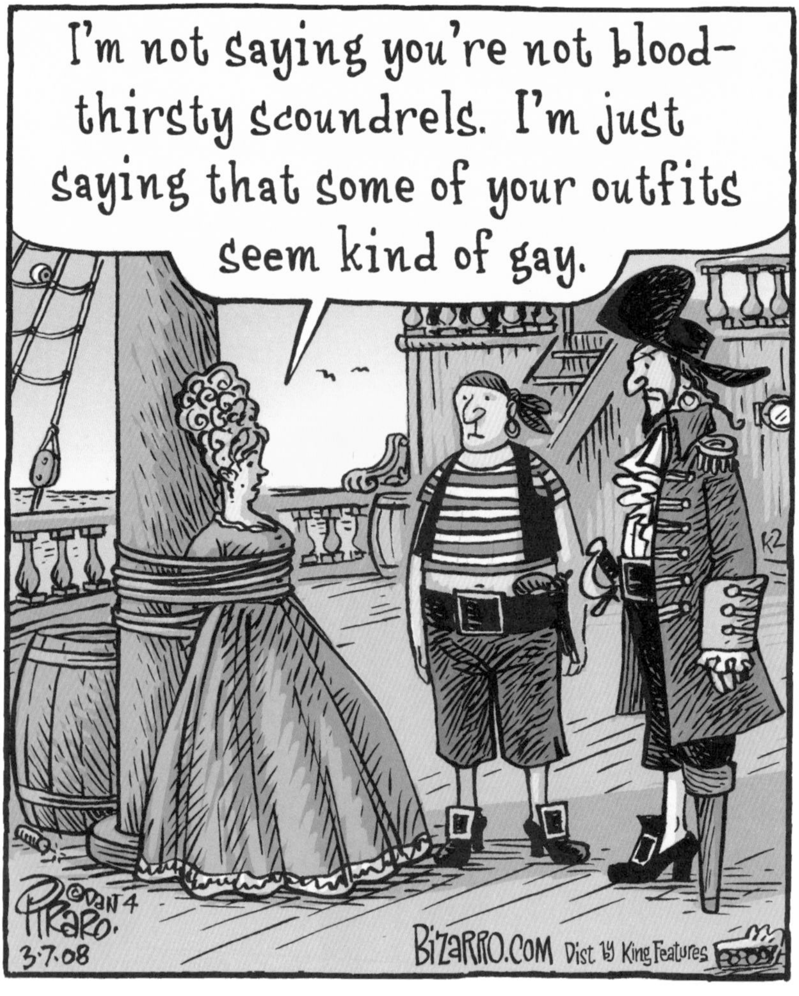

I'm not saying you're not blood-thirsty scoundrels. I'm just saying that some of your outfits seem kind of gay.
©DAN PIRARO 3·7·08
BIZARRO.COM Dist. by King Features

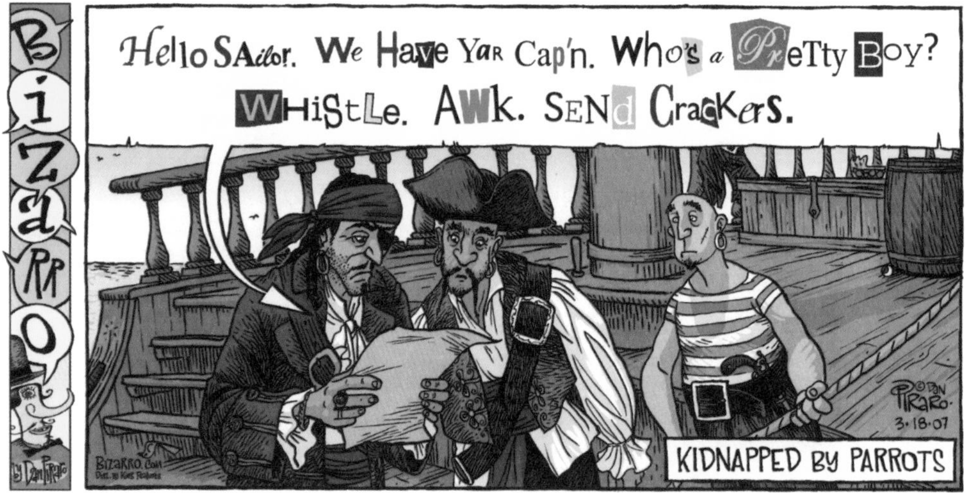
Bizarro
by Dan Piraro
Hello Sailor. We Have Yar Cap'n. Who's a Pretty Boy? Whistle. Awk. Send Crackers.
© Dan Piraro 3-18-07
Bizarro.com
KIDNAPPED BY PARROTS

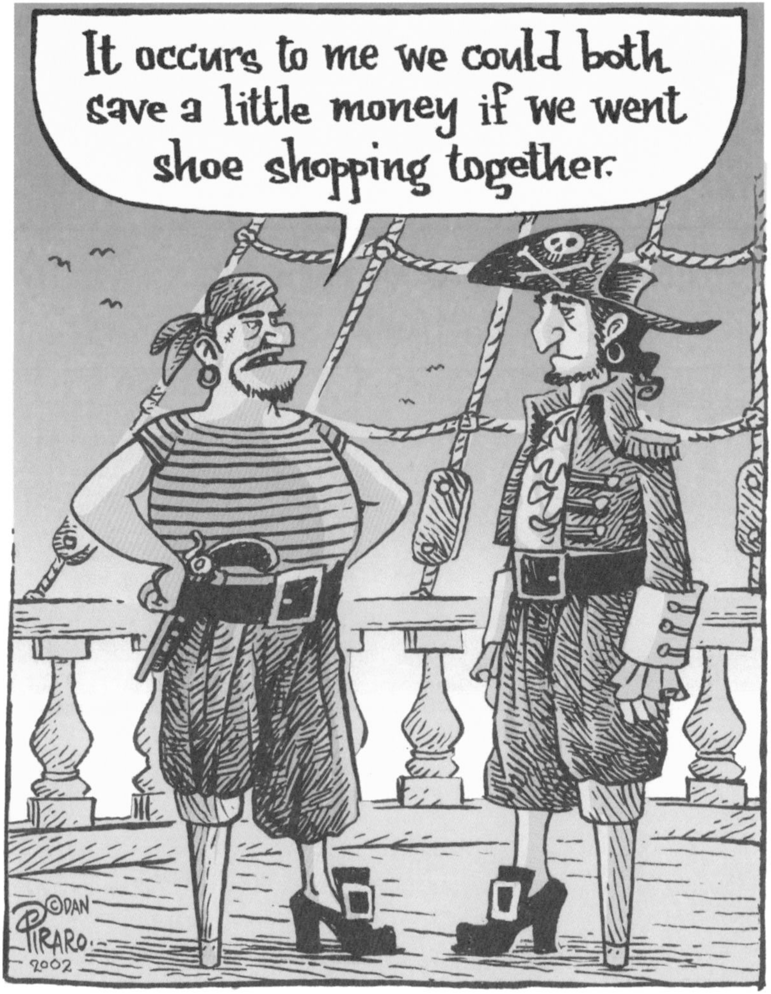
It occurs to me we could both save a little money if we went shoe shopping together.
©DAN PIRARO 2002

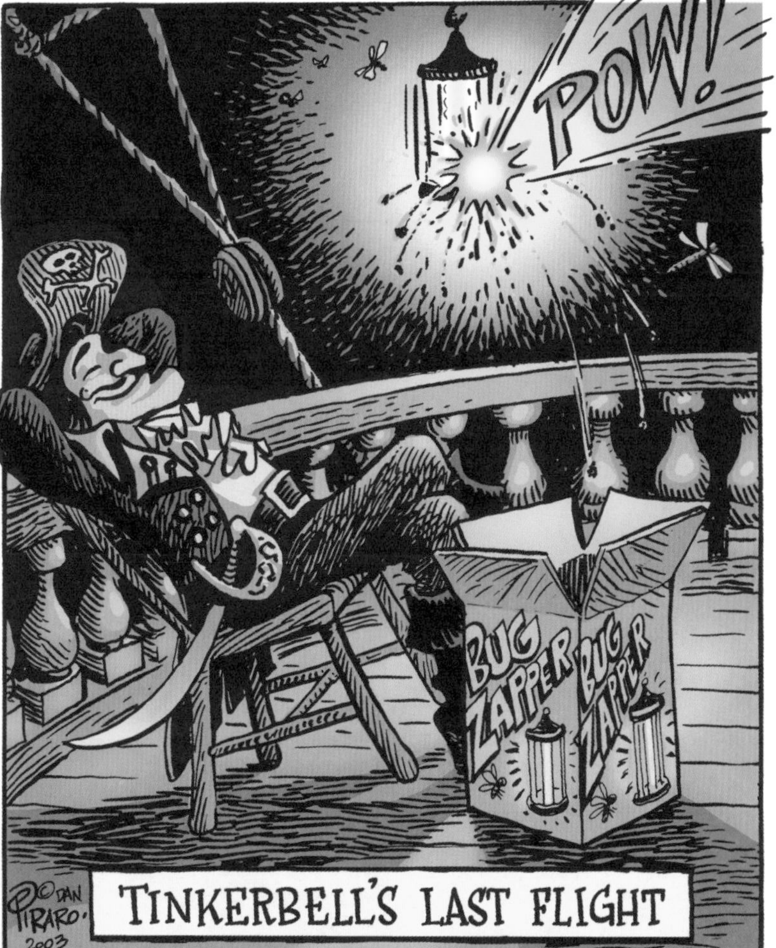
POW!
BUG ZAPPER
BUG ZAPPER
© DAN PIRARO 2003
TINKERBELL'S LAST FLIGHT

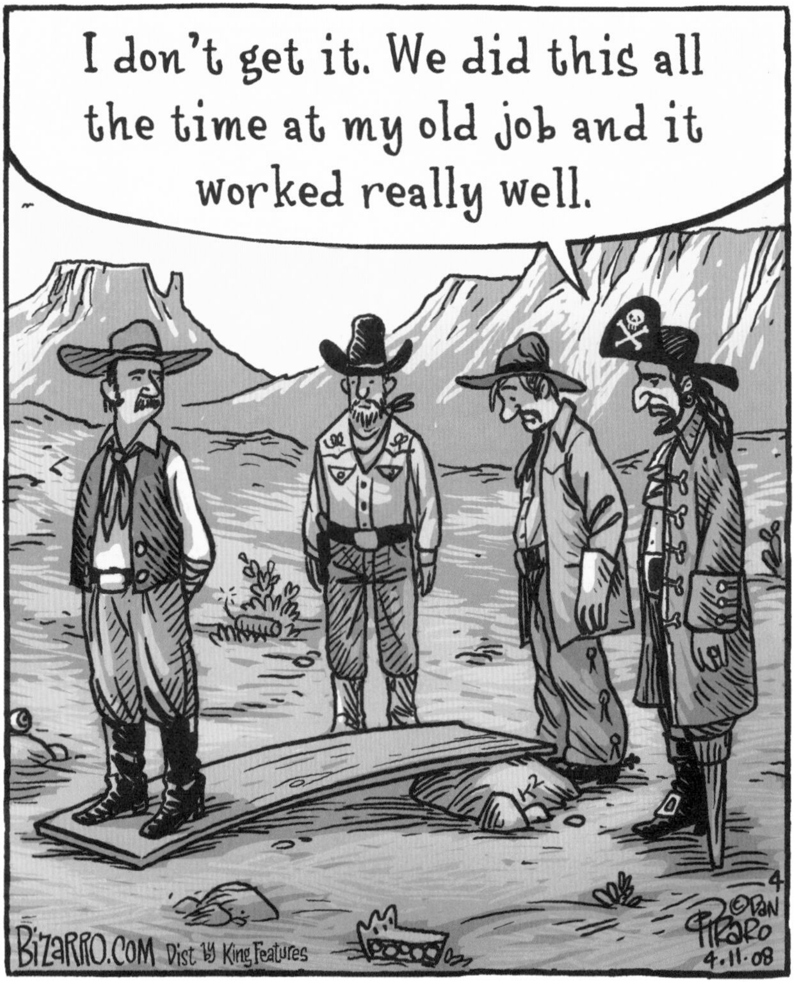
I don't get it. We did this all the time at my old job and it worked really well.
K2
BIZARRO.COM Dist. by King Features
©DAN PIRARO 4.11.08